THE ADDICTION MANIFESTO

By JR Weaver

Charleston, SC
www.PalmettoPublishing.com

The Addiction Manifesto
Copyright © 2021 by JR Weaver

All rights reserved

No portion of this book may be reproduced, stored in a retrieval system, or transmitted in any form by any means–electronic, mechanical, photocopy, recording, or other– except for brief quotations in printed reviews, without prior permission of the author.

First Edition

Paperback ISBN: 978-1-63837-763-4
eBook ISBN: 978-1-63837-349-0

Library of Congress Control Number: 2021912519

This book is dedicated to

To those amazing individuals that never stopped believing in me, without you I wouldn't be here.
Thank you.

CUNNING, POWERFUL, BAFFLING

If *only* it was about not using (abstinence)—but it's deeper than that, smarter than that. Addiction is way more cunning. It's in a state of constant evolution; it uses everything to twist our reality to serve its purpose. Addicts want to quit, but the guilt/shame/hopelessness/trauma/desperation keeps us in a state of despair. We seek escape from reality because dealing with reality and the consequences of our past actions is frightening. Who wants to admit they screwed up their life? Who wants to admit they lost control? Addiction plays on our fears to keep us prisoners. I know this to be the ugly truth because it kept me a prisoner to my own fears for years. We each have the key to our freedom, but how many of us are ready to face life on life's terms? If I told you that society wants you back, would you listen? If I told you that your family still loves you, would you hear me? Addiction never loved you; it played you, like it played me and countless others, but there is a way out that many of us have learned. All you need to do is believe in yourself and show up each day to get better. Whenever I write, I always hope that my message reaches the people who need to hear what I am saying—because I've been where you're at, and I know how it feels to be broken. But today, I know how it feels to not be afraid of sharing my testimony from my journey to hell and back.

Hello, my name is JR Weaver, and I'm a person in lifetime recovery from drugs and alcohol. I am an army veteran, certified peer-support specialist, senior mentor for Veteran's Treatment Court, and an employee at our local

VA hospital working in the sterile processing department. I am not a writer by choice but by necessity because my own sobriety depends on it. Writing helped me during some of the most desperate moments of my life; it helped me dissect what my addiction was feeding me and what my addiction was doing to me. For about twenty years, I ran the streets. I have been homeless, hopeless, godless, and just "lost" to the reality that my life was worth anything more than the next hit or drink. That is exactly what substance use disorder does to us—it blinds us to the reality or reasons behind why our lives have become unmanageable and spiraled out of control. It breaks us down from the inside out, piece by piece, until there is nothing "original" left inside us. It will take us away from everything and everyone who might cause us to rethink our choices. It must isolate us from the voice of reason until the only voice we hear is the voice of addiction. Then it owns us.

My story is filled with ugly memories of times when I tried to fight back but ended up in the same place. Addiction knows that all it had to do is wait patiently for us to do that next "hit," and we are right back to doing its ugly bidding. I am a guy who needed help but didn't know how to ask for help. Being a veteran, I wasn't accustomed to showing weakness, so I bottled up everything, and my life soon revolved around alcohol and drugs. I lost control and was stuck in a never-ending, self-destructive cycle that was going to kill me if I didn't change.

After hitting my last rock bottom and facing felony charges in two counties, I found myself at the lowest point in my life. I needed help because everything I'd tried failed. I pleaded into drug court on November 15, 2017, and thought I would just do the year to clear my charges. I didn't have a "solid" recovery plan, so guess what happened next? Four more felony charges from another county popped up on the radar from my last relapse. The part I want to drive home is that I had a choice to make back then, over 2018 New Year's weekend (of course, it had to be the biggest party weekend of the year). I could take the little bit of cash I had to go get high, or I could save it for canteen when the police came. I decided to stay sober through the holiday weekend and make it to work on Tuesday to learn that the police had also checked there for me on Friday. Well, it didn't take a rocket scientist to figure out the VA police were trying to indiscreetly follow me to detain me for the police, so I had another "moment of truth."

I could run, or I could get my affairs in order for what was to come. I sat there at our break table, knowing they were coming, and took the few minutes to write down addresses and phone numbers. I was tired of running. I believed that God had a plan, so I sat there waiting. Long story short, I spent ninety days locked up while drug court rolled my new charges into my plea. On day ninety-one, I walked right back to the hospital to resume my treatment program because I knew that was the last thing my addiction thought I would do. I took back my life. I graduated drug court with no sanctions because I believed in the program and really wanted my life back. Guess where I'm employed? The exact same VA hospital where I was shackled hand and foot. I do hope my story helps at least one person. You deserve a better life than you think you do.

> **ONE WAY OR ANOTHER YOUR STORY WILL MAKE A DIFFERENCE. IT CAN BE A GREAT COMEBACK STORY OR ONE WHERE FRIENDS ARE SAYING GOODBYE ON UR TIMELINE. YOUR CHOICE.**
>
> JR WEAVER

WHAT A WICKED WEB WE WEAVE WHEN WE ALLOW OUR ADDICTION TO DECEIVE.

Life is hard. Addiction makes it harder. We tell ourselves anything to make excuses for our dark behavior. If we can lie to ourselves, then lying to anybody else becomes second nature. I have lied, cheated, and stolen to feed my addiction. Each time, it got easier because I was slowly losing faith in myself, piece by piece. I was selling my soul to keep the drugs coming, so I couldn't feel anything inside. I hated myself, and I blamed everyone *but me* for making this monster. Recovery has opened my eyes to where I was and has given me a chance at a truly amazing life. It hasn't been easy by any means. *Recovery takes effort.* Do I go to every meeting with a big smile on my face? No. Some days, I just want to skip the meeting and do other things. Although I may drag my feet going to a meeting, I usually leave it thankful that I did go. Most times, you will hear something that strikes home and be like, "Wow, I needed to hear that." When I first started going to meetings, I was guilty of not really paying attention to what others were saying. I thought I knew it all. My recovery was weak, and I let my demons break free and eventually relapsed. My last relapse was July 2017, and it didn't last just the planned weekend; it lasted four months. It took every ounce of strength to sober up. Do not ever be afraid to face your demons. To be afraid is exactly what they want you to do; that gives them power over you to keep you enslaved. Find out what keeps you sober and do more of that! Stay proactive. Don't talk about wanting a better life; get out there and put forth the effort to make that happen! This is your life. You decide how you are going to live it: free to choose or chained to a habit that will kill you or jail you. Your choice.

Addiction: Destroying Us from the Inside Out.

Imagine this: something so powerfully deceptive that it blinds us to the chaos that comes with it. We get so blinded by the illusion addiction paints for us that we fail to see all the things it takes from us. We lose "self-control" while doing its bidding, so we lose touch with reality. The reality is that our addiction is stripping everything we love from us: our families, our friends, and sadly, our life.

How do we allow this to happen? For some of us, it's a slow change in behavior. It slowly tears us away from our families and children. How many of you blindly walked out of their lives? We may have started using recreationally, but we are programmed differently: one drink or one drug is all it takes to send us off to the races. We binge, and we binge hard. That's how I was wired, and I'm guessing you were wired this way too. We can't do "just one," so don't ever let your addiction trick you to believing that again. Our addiction is the puppet master; it controlled us to the brink of our own destruction. We all know people who couldn't stop and paid the ultimate price. Somehow those of us in recovery must take the lead and bring others to share the stories that led us to wanting a better life, free from active addiction. I challenge each of you to avoid complacency and reach out to the still-struggling addict. I know ultimately, it's up to them to want recovery, but sometimes, they just need a little push.

Dig Deeper.

AA/NA/CA works. It builds the foundation for a better life. Newcomers to the program often overlook the obvious. It's not about just reading the simple steps; it's about rebuilding your life into something that will always give back to you. It teaches you how to appreciate yourself. When I first entered the doors to AA/NA, I wasn't there for the right reasons. I was there because I was "told" to be there. I rebelled, as some of you might be doing. I wasn't allowing myself a fair chance at receiving what was really being offered: a better life.

I attended about seventy meetings in ninety days and foolishly didn't follow any suggestions and didn't embrace the fellowship. I thought that, since I had a few months of sobriety, that I had beaten my addiction. That was what my ego was telling me. My ego couldn't have been more wrong. Relapse followed. I regret not embracing my recovery from the start, but in reality, that last relapse made me "dig deeper" into my recovery. I lost my ego and fully accepted that I had a serious problem and that I needed help. Everything I'd tried to sober up had failed miserably, and I was more desperate than a drowning man. I opened myself up to my recovery. I had to "dig deeper," so I committed myself to getting better, and the positive results started manifesting themselves. Recovery does nott happen overnight; it's a daily process to rebuild everything that our addiction destroyed. As I approach my first year of sobriety (November 10), I am able to look back at my former self and remember a time not that long ago when I totally believed that I couldn't sober up, when I hated the monster I had become. I had no hope, no faith, and no chance at living a life worth living. Those thoughts are no longer welcome here, but I will keep the memories as fuel to always "dig deeper" in my recovery as if my life and future depended on it—because they do.

I am writing this book to show people that addiction is a serious disease and that it doesn't care about color, gender, religion, or race. What's the easiest way to describe what addiction wants from us? *It wants our Souls!* I'm hoping that my experiences will help fellow addicts regain their life or help enlighten friends and family about what addicts have to deal with on a daily basis. Random House defines addiction as "the state of being enslaved to a habit or practice or to something that is psychologically or physically habit-forming, as narcotics, to such an extent that its cessation causes severe trauma."

Addiction will destroy your life like a wrecking ball; it doesn't care what you have do to feed it. Crimes? Robbing? Stealing? Tricking? It tells *you* to do *whatever* it takes to get that next high. Most of us have seen the dark side of our addiction and what it brings us. The destruction, chaos, and even deaths of people we may have known. We lose our willpower to fight it, and we end up losing ourselves, our families, and maybe even our lives. Why? Why do we have to finally arrive at that make-or-break point to recognize the damage we have inflicted on ourselves, our families, and society? Why wait until we are sick and tired of being sick and tired? Why is it so hard for us to finally reach that first step and admit to ourselves that "Houston, we have a major problem"?

The best answer I can give is that we just didn't know what to do—or maybe we were afraid to do what we needed to do to get help. Part of us still believed the BS that our addiction was feeding us. That the next hit was going to be the hit of hits or that the next drink was going to make all of our problems disappear. That's the *power of our addiction,* and sadly, most of us addicts have been there or know others who have been manipulated into doing anything and everything to keep the drugs coming. One does not control addiction, despite what addiction may lead you to believe.

It will tell you that you're different than all the other drug users or alcoholics. If you think you can play around with drugs or alcohol and not worry about the consequences, then you're only fooling yourself. Most of us addicts believed we were smarter than everybody else, that we were hiding our addiction. News flash: everybody knew we were addicts and that we were using, but they were also hoping and praying that we could snap out of it on our own. We couldn't because we weren't ready; we were still believing what addiction was telling us: that we could slow down or control it. It played us like fools. Obsession with drugs and alcohol led me to always want more, more, and more. There was never enough to satisfy my desire. I could never stop chasing that "next high" because, deep down, I was afraid of being sober and having to deal with the problems that I was running from. I just couldn't live like that anymore. Addiction changes each of us; we literally become monsters, divorced from our true identity.

Now we are at that point in our lives where we must face the reality that *we are drug addicts* and *we cannot control our actions when drugs or alcohol is involved*. One hit or drink, and our lives become unmanageable. We get caught up in that "tunnel vision" where we can only think about one thing and one thing only: getting high. Sound familiar? Once we can accept our personal defects, then we can begin to make the necessary adjustments to start leading a life of normalcy and having a life worth living.

Stressed? Scared? Addiction will control your life. It will destroy all hopes of your future, and it doesn't care. Addiction numbs our hearts to our inner feelings and to the harm we may be doing to others. It will lead us down a path where we may feel unworthy to give and receive love. So what do we do? We do more drugs to keep our minds and hearts from feeling anything. When our tolerance level increases, we just adjust by doing more drugs! Addiction promises us escape from the pain inside, but we lose so much in the process. We lose us. We lose our lives. We lose our families, our children, our self-respect. It destroys each of us from the inside out. We sacrificed our beliefs, principles, families—and for what? Did any of us actually gain anything in our darkest of days? Pain? Jail? Loneliness? We could have ended up losing everything that was important to us. The insanity is real. Addiction is a taker. It will take everything we value in our life; nothing is off limits. Nothing!

We must never doubt that our addiction seeks to control us; a few unfortunate newcomers may not totally accept this truth, yet. For some of us, it was a gradual process through which we were blinded by the addiction fog that blurs our vision to the real world. You (yes, you!) might be a newcomer to this dark world of addiction, and you may still believe you're different that the rest of us. It might take you another year, or maybe five years, to hit rock bottom. Addiction is cunning like this. Its patience is phenomenal; its customizes a personal relapse plan for each of us.

Sometimes, it will move slowly to let you think you're above all of this. Most of us have faced these demons in our past, and we were oblivious to the fact that our addiction was making a power play to consume our lives. We were slowly dying inside, so we continued to self-medicate. We no longer tried to slow down, and we no longer cared what other people thought about us. We had a one-way ticket to self-destruction and no longer cared what happened to us. Sound familiar? We now looked at the world differently; everything was now judged according to getting high and feeding our addiction so we could keep this false feeling.

We don't care about others or the harm to our personal relationships. Do you remember feeling like this? How did you treat your family? Children? I didn't care what they thought about my new behavior. My thinking was that they could believe whatever they wanted. Meanwhile, I kept telling myself that I was in control of my addiction and I could stop anytime. Now sobriety has proved to me that I was living in a fantasy world. I wasn't in control; I couldn't stop on my own. *This* is what you need to believe in *now*. You can't be in control of your addiction; it's too strong, too smart, and too much for you, me, all of us. If you go back out "there," you will be lost again. And maybe this time, you won't be able to bounce back. We are so far down that damn rabbit hole that only a miracle can save us. Sound hopeless? Hell no. You can fix your life by beating addiction, but only if *you* really want it. Do you?

No more! Believe in yourself, look in the mirror, and tell yourself that you can do this! Yes, sobriety is great, but let's talk recovery. Recovery will open your eyes and heart to a life that is amazing. You learn to be happy again, you laugh again, and you have fun again! I was telling my amazing friend that I didn't want a *normal* life. I didn't take on my demons and rebuild my life to just be *normal*—I want *incredible*. Battling addiction makes you such a warrior. You took back your life, and that's some epic Spartan-warrior stuff that makes you strong inside. This real-life stuff that comes at you next is playground stuff. You got this!

BE STRONG ENOUGH TO STAND ALONE, SMART ENOUGH TO KNOW WHEN YOU NEED HELP, AND BRAVE ENOUGH TO ASK FOR IT.

Your willingness to look at your darkness is what empowers you to change.

Scared to Live, Scared to Die

How do we maintain recovery? Beginning in recovery, we often tend to isolate ourselves from having a life. We may work, and we may do the meetings, but afterward, we go home and stay alone for fear of going outside. We feel safe inside, and we may be afraid that, if we go outside, we will be triggered by something or someone. We don't yet believe that we can be saved, and we have not had a chance to fully understand what we need to do in recovery. We have started to hit the meetings, and we have read the twelve steps, but we just don't know how those words can heal us.

Our addiction wants us to have these lingering doubts in the back of our minds because our addiction is already planning our next relapse. When I first started to hit the meetings, I went in *thinking* I could do this. Today, I *know* I can do this. Don't just read the words in each step; dig deeper into the meaning behind each step. Ask somebody that has worked the steps to work with you so you can fully understand what each of them actually means. Let go of your ego and learn humility. We must admit that we don't have a clue how to get better but stay motivated to get better. Learn to trust the process of recovery and the fellowship of AA/NA members who are willing to take a newcomer under their guidance, instead of thinking you know it all and then going home to fight your demons alone. Addiction wins if we allow it to change our homes to solitary prisons. We may feel like we don't deserve a life. I fear this is where some get bored and soon end up going back outside, vulnerable to their demons. Boredom is a trigger. We can't expect a high recovery success rate if we find our recovery boring. What's the point of sobering up to be miserable? How can we find safe, positive, outdoorsy type things to do?

During my early recovery, I had to step outside my comfort zone and try new things. It served two purposes. One, it gave me some new challenge to accomplish while also keeping my mind occupied, and two, it made me feel better. One of the early recovery goals is to build back your self-confidence so you feel better about yourself. Do not underestimate the value of building yourself up. Those who step outside their comfort zones are more likely to stay in recovery—versus those that lock themselves in their rooms. This past summer, I took my own advice and went out of my own comfort zone. I've taken a summer sea kayaking class and a sailing class over the summer. Guess what happened? I had fun and met new people that I still chat with today. Next up is zip lining and surfing.

During our dark days, we ignored everything but feeding that insatiable beast inside us, and we paid a heavy toll in misery. How about doing something outside your box that will feed your soul? If we can identify those things that have a negative effect and remove them from our life, guess what we end up replacing them with? Things that are positive and good for us, things that make us feel good inside. Soul food—that's one of my personal goals of recovery.

> Watching someone you love destroy themselves is heartbreaking, but imagine being the person that is hurting the people they love by being unable to stop, thats the reality that so many of us struggle with every day.
>
> JR WEAVER

Accept life on your 'new' lease. Sobriety has saved us from our demons, but if we don't learn from our past, if we don't keep progressing in our daily recovery, then how can we really be ready for what life is going to throw at us? Yes, it's a blessing to finally sober up, but now we have to learn to deal with life, and that's a beautiful thing despite the many obstacles that we will now have to face. We can no longer believe that we can ignore everything we blew off in the past. Accountability in our new lease on life is just one major step to fully healing ourselves.

We go to work to earn money to pay for our past transgressions. Yes, society wants payback. We may face dealing with medical or family obligations that we blew off during our addictions. Life isn't going to just welcome us back with a sunshine-paved road. Real life is tough, but so are you. You survived addiction's best shot, so take pride in yourself. Don't get overwhelmed by what life is throwing at you; take it one day at a time and focus on improving yourself daily. That's how we conquer our past and move forward to a better life. I went from waking up before the sunrise to walking to catch the first of two buses to get to work; rain or shine, I made the mile walk. It wasn't easy, but I accepted that it was going to be a struggle, and you know what? It got easier. I finally got a car. Life does get better; the thoughts and cravings and dreams do eventually go away. Believe you can do it and just go do it. For yourself. Then everything else will fall into place.

Ask for help and commit yourself to your recovery! Take responsibility for your own recovery. Have faith that you can make it, that you will be a success. People like you and me are rewriting history every day. Believe in us; believe we can overcome anything that addiction throws in our path. Do not hold back in your recovery and never let your addiction trick you into letting your guard down. Remember that it's always out there waiting and plotting a way to get us back under its control. We need to stay proactive in our recovery because we have learned what happens when we don't.

Give yourself the best chance at having a life. Do this for yourself, and everything else will fall into place. A few of you may have been struck down overnight and lost everything. I can only pray that something in these pages touches each of you so you will be motivated to take a hard, honest look at your life right now. I am writing this to give each of you hope and faith that you can turn your life around. I am writing to starve your addiction and feed your recovery. It can be done, but first, you need to recognize the power of addiction and admit that you have a problem. Yes, I have a problem with drugs and alcohol; you have a problem with drugs and/or alcohol. Are you ready to take back your life?

Stared into the Abyss,
Nearly lost myself,
But in my darkest hour,
I truly found myself

> To find **peace**, you have to be willing to lose your connection with the people, places, and things that create all the noise in your life.
>
> unknown
> livelifehappy.com

I've been battling *my demons* for over twenty years. I would have brief moments of sobriety, but eventually, my addiction would always come back stronger than ever to kick my teeth in. The relapse would always take it up another level. Eventually, I would have to sober up; maybe the money or drugs would slow down, and I would find myself hating the life I was leading. I would go into treatment or try to sober up on my own. But the result was always the same: relapse. We can't think that we're *miraculously* cured just because we're not using or the cravings have vanished. Abstinence from using is almost always temporary; we have to keep adjusting our game plan to stay ahead of addiction. What do you think your addiction is doing right now? You might feel safe that the thoughts of using and the cravings have slowed down, but guess what? Your addiction isn't gone; it's regrouping; it's in the gym, lifting weights; it's reviewing the game tapes, and it's already planning your next relapse!

That's addictions modus operandi. To get you to relax in your recovery and wait patiently on the sidelines for just the sliver of an opening. Then it comes back stronger than ever. I can tell you this is real talk; the next time, you may not only lose your freedom; you may lose your life. The best weapon against addiction? To not challenge it to a fight, I have seen it knock out the strongest of people; it wants you to start thinking that you're stronger, faster, and smarter than before. We can only win by avoiding it altogether. Do not think you can pick up a drink or take a hit; you can't, I can't, none of us can. We are addicts, and all it takes is that first one to get us to scrap everything and be right back where we left off.

Stay out of the ring and work on staying sober daily. Keep your recovery strong and stay active with whatever works for you. If attending and sharing at meetings keeps you sober, then keep doing that. Find what works for you and never get complacent in your recovery; this game of life and death is always changing for us. It only takes a few minutes of some seriously bad thinking to screw up everything! What works for me might not work for others, but each addict has to truly covet their own sobriety. We may want to get clean for other reasons, like for family, but we have to accept that, if we do it for ourselves, then everything else will fall back into place. That's the ultimate blessing of recovery—when our lives start to get better. Talk is cheap in this war against addiction. Action is what matters the most—staying sober, stacking clean days, and building a new sober lifestyle. We have to learn to rebuild our social network. Those old friends and places that always caused us to relapse? Gone! We can't expect to change our lifestyle if we're still hanging out with those people or in those places. It doesn't work. We have to learn to remove those negative things from our life and replace them with positive things. What happens when we do that? We find we have all this extra time to do positive things, things that bring us joy and happiness and that will help us stay sober.

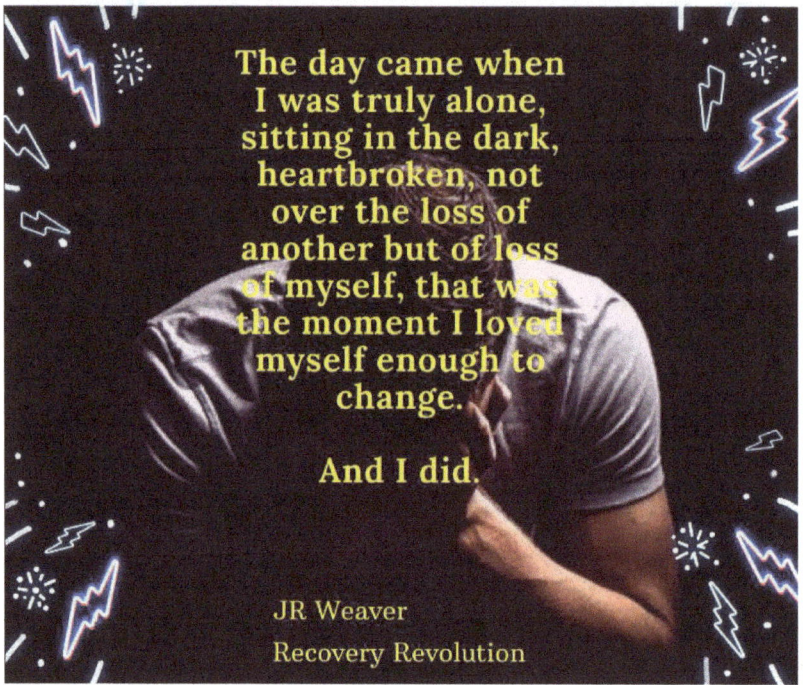

Today, I am grateful for my sobriety and strong recovery program that is giving me the chance to have a wonderful life. All I wanted was a chance to do things differently this time, and I've been blessed to have this chance. You can have the same opportunity, but it's not going to happen without your total commitment.

ONE DAY AT A TIME!

Hello, my name is JR Weaver, and I'm a recovering addict and alcoholic. Over the last twenty-seven years, I have tried just about every drug under the sun: coke, heroin, weed, meth, mushrooms, molly, x, Special K. I've lied, cheated, stolen, bought the t-shirt, and then traded it on the way to finance my growing addiction. My addiction has led to countless times behind bars and nearly cost me all my familial and personal relationships. Please do not let my past mislead you, despite my epic failures at trying to stay clean. My past helped shape who I am today, but by no means does it define who I am today. To judge or label me based on my past mistakes is your option, of course, but you would be missing out on a great comeback story about how I am going to beat this addiction and return to a life worth living. I truly believe that I am blessed to have another chance at doing the right thing.

For twenty-seven years, I have chased something that has used and abused me a hundred times over. It "played" me, changed me, and nearly destroyed me. Addiction is a sneaky, powerful, and baffling enigma; it wants to isolate you, it wants to be your only, friend, and it will promise you the moon and the stars. But it will deliver nothing short of a train-wrecked life. It's miserable being a drug addict; your only friends are other addicts, who will sell you out for their next high, or dealers, who really only want your money. This is my story, my journey on my road to recovery. What I learned about addiction, the mind games it plays on us, and the ways we can stay sober.

We have to learn to stay a few steps ahead because life isn't going to be easy, and it's so easy to fall back into what we know: drugs and addiction. People in recovery are warriors! We have a fight to take back our lives, and we won't surrender. Most of us are just tired of being "sick and tired" and want something, anything, to take away this sickness. We can only keep what we have by giving it away, so I am writing this to help myself stay sober, and hopefully my story will encourage other addicts to take a look at their lives. I started writing this journal while sitting behind bars for four burglary charges—thanks to my addiction. I was arrested at the VA hospital and was shackled to do the "walk of shame" to the police car.

Jan 2, 2018—helluva way to start the new year off, right? This story came from my heart. I bled for this story and almost lost the next ten years of my life behind bars for doing something that would feed my addiction! I couldn't live like this anymore. I wanted more out of "me," and getting locked up or being stuck in some crappy motel room, secretly hating the monster that I had become, wasn't going to work. My addiction fought me for my soul, but I was finally seeing a way out of its tentacles. I just needed to stay sober and find out what worked for me. Thankfully, I had entered the Charleston County Drug Court Program prior to my incarceration, and they really helped me out. I owe them a huge debt for "saving" me.

How am I doing today? I'm free of active addiction; sobriety has opened so many doors that I once believed were closed to me. I'm happy, employed, and rebuilding my life the way I want it. I'm finally in control of my future. This "personal" book is based on my experiences and my thoughts about what was happening inside my head during my active addiction and also now as I am working on my recovery. You have a chance to take back control of your life and get back everything and more, but you really have to want to make that happen. You can't *half-ass* recovery; there is no *easier, softer way* to do recovery if you expect to stay sober. I tried it and was back out on the streets before long. Commit yourself totally; those thoughts in the back of your mind whispering to you that I don't know what I am talking about—what do you think they are? That's your addiction; it knows you're on the verge of doing something positive that will let you break free from its hold. You're at the intersection of recovery or addiction. Which way will you go?

There is no person on this earth, who exhibits more strength, courage, and dignity on a daily basis than an addict in recovery.

I can choose to let it
define me, confine me,
refine me, or outshine me,
or I can choose to move on
and leave it behind me.

tinybuddha.com

You! Yes, you! Yes, we made mistakes in the past; we are all human. What matters is that we picked ourselves up and learned from our mistakes! *People in recovery are warriors.* We didn't give up when the odds were against us; we battled back to stand here today, clean and sober. That's something that all of us can take pride in.

One key point to consider is that you have to actually be in recovery to relapse. What is recovery? Recovery is being abstinent from all drugs and alcohol, working on changing your behavior (and thoughts) to become a better person (mentally, physically, and spiritually), and leading a life worth living. Just because you survived your past doesn't mean you should consider yourself safe from future relapse. Just because you have maintained sobriety for multiple years doesn't mean you're invincible either. Less than a one third of people entering recovery will make it a year. Our addiction may lie dormant, but it's not resting; it's hitting the weights and planning on you coming back. If we don't embrace the full program of recovery, the well-balanced life that is constantly improving (mentally, socially, physically, spiritually), then we leave ourselves open to relapse. Did my God save me from the destruction yesterday to watch me fall tomorrow? No. He saved me to live a life less ordinary, to be happy, to smile more and help others. Have I solved my addiction? No. But I will continue to lead a positive life that will help keep me safe from relapse.

Relapse can begin before any drug or alcohol has hit the body. My last relapse (which was a doozy) started way before I picked up the phone to call my dealer (and yes, I know I should have deleted all my old phone numbers, and thanks to Lauren Nelson's pushing me, I now have no numbers in my phone from that part of my life). I had managed to get four months sobriety with about seventy meetings in about ninety days (high five), but I started working two jobs for about sixty hours a week, so my attendance at meetings started to diminish.

I had applied to drug court around this time and knew that, if I could just make it to drug court, I would be safe, but I made a mistake and let my addiction start whispering in my ear about how, *if* I was going to relapse, I'd better do it before I commit to drug court. The early warning signs were flashing bright, but I ignored them. I was going strong, right? Well, the two jobs finally started to take their toll on me. My stress levels started to rise, and I was still skipping meetings. I forgot to mention that I was staying in a homeless shelter at this time too. I finally found an apartment that I could rent. Someone was willing to take a chance on an ex-con with a history of addiction. I should have realized how blessed I was to get the opportunity. I didn't. The seeds of my destruction had already been planted in my mind, without me catching them. My addiction was steadily working me, telling me how strong I was now, how much I had changed. It led me to the thought that I could control my usage. I bought into the story and called my dealer. One gram wouldn't hurt, right? Who would know? That one gram turned into about four months of using before I realized that I'd just gotten "got!" We fail to realize how our addiction is a master manipulator; it could probably sell ice to an Eskimo. My binge led me to losing both jobs and my apartment, and I caught four burglary charges. That's what addiction does!

Addiction will toy with our feelings about guilt or shame, but check this out: all of us have done things in our past that we're not proud of, and we can live a life of regret, or we can somehow make amends and get past our mistakes. We cannot live in the past if we want to move forward into the future. We have to catch the early warning signs before they can get a foothold in our brains. All it takes is for us to let our defenses down or allow ourselves to start believing the hype that we are cured. How many times can we fall for the same Jedi mind tricks? We admitted we were powerless over alcohol and sought help from our higher power, but if we don't do any recovery or any routine recovery maintenance, then it's only a matter of time before we let our addiction take control again. We let ourselves get so busy in our "new" lives that we forget what gave us the chance to have those lives. Sobriety and recovery. We have to change our lifestyle and the way we think. Otherwise, we have learned nothing, and we're doomed to repeat the same mistakes again. Do not make the same mistakes that I did; do the work on your recovery, figure out the early warning signs, and develop a plan of action. Attend the meetings. You might not need what they are offering now, but you might just need it six months from now. Work your recovery plan, develop a relapse prevention plan, and remember to take time out for yourself by doing something you enjoy, whether it's spending time shopping, with family, hitting the gym, or reading a book. You need your very own personal time.

Acceptance

Everybody has their own opinions on drug and alcohol addiction, but until you've been there, your opinion is just that: your opinion. Yes, they chose to abuse drugs or alcohol, thinking they would be able control it. You don't control a drug; it controls you. There are some lucky ones who have beaten it, but don't think, because they're still alive, that life is gravy. They fight every day, all day, to stay clean or sober. It's a constant battle from the time they open their eyes to when they close them, and it never goes away. Most are good people who made a bad choice. Some may have started in their earlier years and thought they were immune to the dangers. Maybe they thought they were just different from all the other people they'd seen on the streets. Battling a drug or alcohol addiction is a beast for the people addicted and the ones who love them. So, this is in loving memory of every family member and friend who has lost their battle with drugs and alcohol, as well as those who continue to struggle against it. Drug and alcohol addiction is the abyss.

A friend overdosed yesterday and I'm trying to sort through this roller coaster of emotions. I know we can't save everyone from their demons, but it still doesn't stop the "what if" questions from rattling around my head. He was doing so well; he'd been sober for a few months, and this was totally unexpected. He was only nineteen years old and had a life ahead of him. This shows me that addiction doesn't care who you are, what part of town you're from, who your parents are; it wants what it wants, when it wants it. I feel torn inside for not reaching out, but how could I have known? What possessed him to do what he did? We can never be completely safe from relapse, and we never know what the outcome will be either. I mentioned earlier that we all have the potential for another relapse, but we may not have another recovery in us. I don't think he had any children, but I know he had a mother and a father who loved him. Think about what you do and the potential consequences. I know some of you have children, spouses, and family members who love you unconditionally, so how do you think they would be able to cope with losing you? Is a quick high worth the potential damages? Are you willing to risk everything that you may have gained? Jail or death—that's what is out there for us, and I'm not willing to risk either to feed something that causes me nothing but misery.

I think back to my "dark years" and how I treated people who only wanted to help me; it's a sad life we live as addicts. We forget who we really are, who we really care about. Addiction is a savage; it just doesn't care about us. It will burn through us until we're dead or incarcerated and then simply move on to the next person, without even looking back at us. Is that what you want for yourself? It makes me angry to think about the years and friendships that I lost over my using. You can't win in this game; addiction holds all the cards, and you will lose everything. Sober up, people! The only way to win is to not play this game with addiction. David, you will be missed, my friend.

Eliminating the negative people, places and things from our lives as we begin our journey toward recovery. We are faced with the familiar faces from our past life, mainly the *people* we may have used with, the *places* we may have used, or the *thing***s** that we may have used. Limiting our contact with these faces from our past is a must if we hope to break those chains that will lead us to relapse. Easier said than done, right? If we truly want to maximize our chances for success, then we must make the tough choices to eliminate those things that lead us back toward the life we want to escape. We must find new "sober" friends who want us to do better. We must find new social activities that are challenging and entertaining. We can't expect to go hang out in the same areas with the same people if we want to change our life. This is our life. I'm sure that, once upon a time, we may have believed we could just stop using and that would be enough. But was it? We gave our addictions so much. We hustled night and day to satisfy this hunger that could not be satisfied. If you were like me, then you tried the easier, softer way, and it backfired; you relapsed. I know I tried everything possible to solve this addiction matrix, and the results sucked until I accepted defeat and admitted I had a major problem. I couldn't beat it on my own; I couldn't control it. I had to break down and finally ask for help. I was just sick and tired of not being in control of my life. Embrace your recovery and go after it with the same hustle with which you went after your addiction.

Recovery isn't for those that need it. Recovery is for those that want it! Change your life; do things that will give back to you! You will find that life has its ups and downs, but special moments every day can put a genuine smile on your face. We can be happy and free from our addiction. It's proven, but it's not going to be easy. Some days, you will question everything. Is it worth it? Has your life improved? I can only speak for myself, but hell yeah. My life is so much better today because I put maximum effort into my recovery. Whatever keeps you sober, do that! Do things that feed your soul, and you will find your very own personal road map to living happy, joyous, and free.

I am not going to blast you with a ton of medical definitions or results from medical research studies. That stuff is great and very helpful for breaking down the inner workings of our disease, but today I am going to break down what I learned about addiction from living on the streets. Each addict is wired differently, but I am positive that most addicts will agree with what I am about to talk about.

> You're always one decision away from a totally different life.
>
> - unknown
>
> Daily Quotes

I believe each of us has to reach that "point" where we openly want sobriety. It took me dozens of attempts at sobriety before I started to realize the patterns that led to my relapses. The addict has to be tired of being controlled by a substance and be willing to work toward recovery. We have to start this process on our own. We have to believe that we can only truly "live" by giving up the things that chained us in the past, our addictions. We seek abstinence and want to be clean and sober. We want to enjoy our life. We're tired of all the lying, stealing, cheating, and living that "life."

We must be willing to ask for help. We have learned in the past that we can't do this alone, but the incredible thing is, we don't have to fight this battle alone. There is help out there in many different forms. AA/NA, VA, hospitals, rehab centers, detox centers, churches, friends, and families—it's amazing the amount of help that is being offered. Why? *Because people want to see us recover!* This is a lifelong process, and it's so easy to loose progress in a few quick minutes, if we are not careful. We all have another relapse in us, but do we have another recovery? Do you accept that you have a problem with drugs? Are you still under the illusion that you can still use and control it? Is the voice inside your head telling you that you're better than this? Don't waste years like I did before you realize how great a person you really are.

We may have tried to stop using on our own and failed. Our lives have become so unmanageable that we're desperate. We may be alone and scared of the prospect that our life has become a train wreck. One of the key beliefs in AA/NA is the belief in a higher power. I believe I am blessed by something greater than myself. How else can I find myself being sober today? What else could have directed me to write this book to help others? I couldn't do it on my own. I have tried numerous times. To the newcomer, the religious side can be scary. We might believe we don't need prayer or a higher power in our life. Where was this higher power when you were down and out? You can believe what you want, but you're here now because something brought you here. Something wants you to change, wants you to beat your addiction. Regular people pray when things in their life go badly. We may not be regular people due to our addiction, but how's life treating you? Your life is in turmoil, so maybe, just maybe, you might want to start believing that there is something out there that will help you on your new path.

We have to admit that we are powerless and that a power greater than ourselves can restore us to sanity. I can't make you believe in religion or a higher supreme being up there in the heaven, and I'm not trying to preach to you, but if we truly want recovery, we have to be willing to go above and beyond. Changing our behavior and thought patterns is great, and we want to build up as much immunity as possible against addiction. You are still alive today, after all that you have been through. You may have seen others overdose and questioned why you're still here. I know I have questioned why I am still here, while other wonderful people are gone. Maybe I am here to help others. If I can help save someone from this life by writing about addiction or stop someone from starting up on the path to addiction, to spare someone from having to endure the same mistakes in life that I have made, then it was worth every moment.

Have faith that you have a guardian angel up there watching over you and that you are being tested with only what you can handle. Think about this: why do you think you are still here after all that you have been through? I have stayed in some of the most dangerous neighborhoods and dealt with the shadiest of people, yet I am still here. I have snorted, smoked, and shot insane amounts of narcotics, yet still, here I am, and here you are too. We have been blessed with another chance at life, and I know for me it's not just a second chance; it's more like my fiftieth second chance to get my life together. I don't think I have another recovery in me, so I am going full throttle to get this thing done right this time, and I hope you are ready to join me on this lifetime journey.

> Losing everything taught me to appreciate life in ways you can't even begin to imagine.
>
> JR WEAVER

Think you're ready for recovery? It was a simple question for me. I wanted a good life, and the only way for that to become reality was to remain sober. I know how my brain and body respond to drugs and alcohol, and it's not good. Some people might be blessed to not have this reaction but for some of us it's a insane reaction that leads us down a dark path. Consider yourself fortunate that you never have been cursed with this affliction. I know from experiments that, if I do one, then I will do many. My binges do not last a night; they last months.

I do not know if I have the inner fortitude for another recovery, and that "fear" drives me to go to insane lengths to make this recovery work. I do not want to lose myself to the streets ever again. I do not want to lose all the positives that I have gained recently. I am finally at a point in my life where I am truly happy, and I know how fast that could deteriorate with just one drink or just one hit. I do not want to be controlled by my addiction ever again. I know my addiction is out there, waiting on me, but gone is the idiotic thinking that I am cured or that I can control my demons. I believe I am a good person inside, and I like "me." I still have the random thoughts pop up inside my head about using, but that's normal because I am human. I'm just a normal guy, trying to stay sober and enjoy life on life's terms.

I accept that there will be ups and downs in my future. That is life. I let my higher power guide me whenever I feel the need for guidance. It's funny how the same issues that we used to hide from during our addiction are very easily dealt with sober. We used to get high to avoid everything, but sober, we are more capable of dealing with the reality of the real world. Addiction doesn't want us to understand that.

"Never give up!"—Winston Churchill

Think addiction is your friend? Addiction does not care if you're tired or hungry or miserable. It has one goal and one goal only: to keep you in active addiction. It drives addicts to keep the "high" going until they literally collapse from exhaustion. It overrides everything in the process. Your body and mind become a empty version of yourself without adequate food or sleep. We are so afraid of missing out on drugs or money (for more drugs) that we do not sleep until we collapse exhausted or get arrested. What kind of friend is that? Do yourself a favor and try to take a break from chasing that high to let your body and mind recharge. You might just discover that the urge or craving to use will go away.

TODAY IS "MY DAY."

Life is a blessing! Sobriety opens our eyes to that. It has its ups and downs, but through recovery, we realize that all the stuff we had to overcome has actually made each of us stronger, so whatever life may throw at us today, we can handle it. A few months back, I accepted that recovery was going to take maximum effort. Out there on the streets, didn't we give 100 percent effort to feeding our addictions? I know I have walked in the darkest hoods in the rain or cold to get my fix, so why wouldn't I do the same to get my recovery? I know life has a way of keeping us so busy that we may start relaxing on our recovery, thinking we're at a "safe place" and do not need to hit the daily meetings or routine recovery maintenance (I am guilty of this too). But we shouldn't forget that we need to stay active in our recovery. It gave us a second chance at life, and I, for one, will never forget that.

Plus, I am scared to death of another relapse. I think we all should be. That's what fuels me each day. No matter how tired or busy I may actually be, I know that, if I start slipping on what got me to where I am now, then I am putting my sobriety and my newfound life in jeopardy. I know I am happy today because I am putting myself into my recovery. I am doing the legwork to stay sober and keep what I have gained. I'm not saying that you have to hit a ton of meetings each week or do a ton of praying, but we have to remember what helped us get sober, and you better believe that our addiction is watching us. It's plotting and scheming. It doesn't like that we are moving on without it, that it's losing its control over us, but you know what I say? Screw addiction! I want better things in my life, and I know for a fact what happens when I let my guard down. Stay focused and on the path, my friends!

> The choices that we each make in life,
> right or wrong, good or bad,
> Own it but don't let it define you.
> Addiction may blur the lines, but
> Sometimes that's exactly what we need
> To appreciate the beauty of recovery.

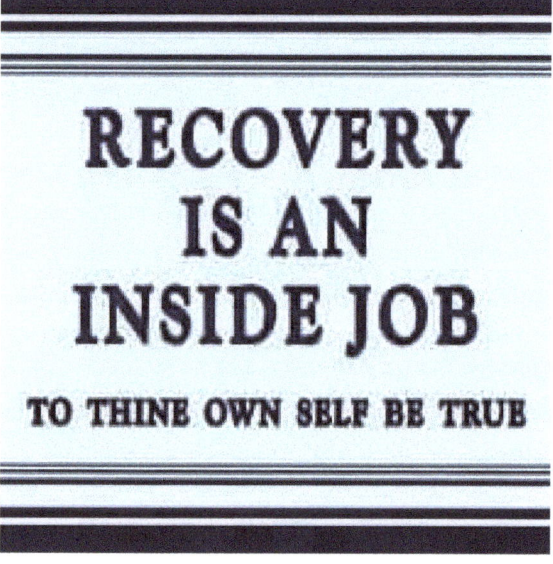

Addiction

Addiction wants your life, your soul. Addiction will change you, jail you, and destroy you. It will wreck your life if you continue to let it. Think about your life, your dreams. Did you ever think you wouldn't be in control of your life? Reality check: on drugs or alcohol, you're not! We all know that *sweet, seductive voice of addiction* that always talked us into doing things we didn't want to do or regretted. It's always whispering things like "Come on, you can have just one drink," or "Come on, treat yourself this weekend; you deserve it." We have all fallen for it time and time again. If you are reading this now, then chances are you have fallen victim to that sweet, seductive voice a few times in your past.

And those people who got high or drunk with you that you called friends? Hate to break it to you, but friends don't let friends destroy their lives. True friends want you to succeed in life. If you're like me, then you've reached a point in your life where you're just tired, physically and mentally. We know what addiction does to us, and we have to want something better in our life, and you can't get better if you continue to use and abuse drugs or alcohol. My desire to have a real life led me to start trying to sober up—and yes, I relapsed a few times along the way. Finally I reached out to the VA's S.T.A.R. (Substance Treatment and Recovery) program; I paid attention in class, learned a lot of new positive things that would help me battle my addiction, and managed to stay clean for a few months this time.

When we break down how addiction works on each of us, we have to acknowledge that addiction is a cunning, powerful, and baffling beast. How many times have we tried to quit on our own? Don't worry. Relapse happens to the even the strongest of us. At least, you're trying to get better, adapt, and overcome. Each time you attempt recovery, it should make your stronger and smarter. It's going to take hard work and a personal commitment to remain sober. It's a long road, but life isn't about crossing the finishing line; it's about what happens along the way. Enjoy every day, even the days you struggle because, at the end, it's all of these tiny moments that reflect your life. We don't have to go back to a life chained to addiction! You can find peace, but you have to be ready to make some life changes! We might believe that it's a sign of weakness to ask for help, but it's not! It's a sign that you're getting stronger. You want to get better, but we both know we can't do this on our own, so ask for help! I did, and it's the best move I have made in years!

Check this out! According to a 2017 World Health Organization survey, about a quarter of a billion people use drugs, and about 29.5 million people have been involved in *problematic use* and suffered from drug use disorders. Opioids were the most problematic of the bunch. Let those numbers sink in for a minute. I am thinking that number doesn't even begin to cover the whole picture because I don't remember any surveys being passed around when I was out there on the streets.

Don't forget the undocumented addicts out there who haven't joined any treatment groups. That's insane! I believe we all have a role to play to help others. Drugs and alcohol are at the top of the list because they create physical, emotional, and social dependence on artificially induced feelings. We believe these feelings are helping us temporarily; we believe the lies that our growing addiction is feeding us. We fail to see the signs that our addictions are slowly taking over our minds. How long before our addictions consume all of our thoughts, time, and energy? Our tolerance levels to reach that same "high" are growing steadily, so we require more and more drugs or alcohol to get that same feeling, right? We are being forced to cover up our old problems with new problems. We do not want to admit that we have a problem. Somehow, we still believe that we are still in control.

It gets so bad that we start lying to cover things up, and how does this affect our current lives? It's slowly destroying us day by day. We stop talking to our friends and families, who only want us to get some type of treatment. *We are living a lie that we believe.* The consequences of our actions are destroying us slowly, and we may end up losing our jobs, our health, our reputations, and our self-respect. We can't control it. Our addictions made us believe otherwise, but how can we stay in denial when our lives are being centered around our addictions? We may decide to slow down our usage to prove to ourselves and others that we are in control and they don't understand what we are going through. The truth is, we may be able to slow down or stop for a few days, weeks, or months, but without a proper recovery program, we will probably fail. These are the binges that we get lost in for a weekend, a week, or maybe months. I know my binges usually last until I get arrested.

> **THE DAY I FINALLY 'OWNED' MY PAST WAS THE DAY IT CEASED 'OWNING' ME.**
>
> *JR Weaver*

No More "Just One More!"

The complexity of addiction to our brains and bodies involves the compulsive use of one or more substances with an absolute disregard for the damage to our health and to our fading social circumstances. Socially, we tend to break off contact from everyone who was in our life previously. This can be our decision—or their decision to distance themselves from us. We as addicts often overlook the isolation we accept. Who do we socialize with after that? Most times, it's other people dealing with their own active addictions. That's how our addiction works to keep us: divide and conquer. Our addiction wants to take us away from the people who truly want to help us.

We all have seen the overwhelming destructive power of our addiction. The chaos, the loss of will power to fight it, the complete and absolute surrender to do what it wants, when it wants. One of the goals of our addiction is to keep us alone so we are vulnerable to its suggestions. This reminds me of a recent Animal Planet show about tigers and how they try to isolate one of the herds of buffalo so they can use their sheer force of numbers to bring the buffalo down.

That's what happens to you, me, and anyone else who allows our addiction to separate us from our families and society. That's the beauty of the fellowship of AA or NA—other recovering addicts that want to see you succeed in beating your active addiction. Yesterday, I went to my very first "sober picnic" after a Sunday-morning meeting. (Thank you, John and Pat, for hosting, and I look forward to next year!) I didn't know what to expect. Maybe ten to twenty people from the meeting rooms? To my surprise, it was about fifty people! We grilled hamburgers and hot dogs, and it was a great time! I met so many new people. It was incredible. I mention this because I know how it is when you start your own recovery. We have spent years isolating ourselves during our addiction; now that we're on the right path to recovery, we often find ourselves isolating ourselves again. Being newly sober and finding yourself alone because you don't know where to meet new people that share your new sober lifestyle is dangerous.

This is where AA/NA can be super helpful. One of my earlier thoughts, back when I was new to the whole meeting concept, was that these people actually wanted to see me do good. They took a real interest in helping others new to the program. They say that the new person is the most important person in the room, and it's true. Get to a meeting early or stay a few minutes after and meet some people. Some of these people have been working the AA/NA program for years and years, so they have seen us newbies come and go. They understand what we are dealing with, and they understand that we're battling a disease that doesn't want to let us go. They are there to help, and all we have to do is listen and absorb what they are telling us. We don't have to battle our addiction on our own. There are so many wonderful support groups out there. So many new sober activities that we should be open to. We have seen how isolation works on us; it leaves us alone to deal with our demons, and that's not a good place to be. Feeling alone in your sobriety and recovery isn't good. What's the point in letting things build up inside our heads about how alone we currently are? My advice is to get active in finding others that share your passion for a better way of life.

Seeing our past self in the faces of a newcomer. One of the cliches of AA/NA is that the newcomer is the most important person in a meeting. Let's take a moment to analyze the real meaning of this by looking at how the newcomer could be us and that addiction is still very real. Yes, I do believe we owe it to them to help them find the gift of recovery, but how far do we go? Granted the newcomer must be open for advice and willing to accept it and practice it. Is that the deepest reason why the newcomer is so vital to us? I'm going to say no. Let me explain before you start throwing stones at me. I sat in a vet meeting today, and we discussed how one of our brothers had relapsed over the weekend. Relapse happens to a bunch of us. Sometimes, it's part of the process to shake loose those last threads of doubt about being stronger or being able to control your addiction; we can't ever allow our minds to think this way. So when I was hearing the story, I thought about my buddy who had relapsed recently. I remembered the look in my friend's eyes: shame, guilt, embarrassment, fear. Relapse is common, but two positive things happened: I saw my old self in him, and it made me realize it could have been me. Hell, that was me just eleven to twelve months ago, and realizing that strengthened my own recovery because I'm never going back to that lifestyle. Two, it opened my buddy's eyes to how fast your past can become your present. I believe it motivated him to take his recovery seriously. Is it wrong for someone's relapse to boost recovery? No, we have been there, and I hope my last relapse strengthened another person's recovery, just as my friend's did mine. We see our old selves in the faces of the newcomers, and we know what they are dealing with. Our job is to help guide them along this path to recovery, hoping they really want it and make the effort to go get it. The spirituality part of step 12 is what I refer to as enlightenment. We have been blessed with the vision to see what addiction has done and what it's trying to manipulate to get us back. We understand addiction and the dangers that come with it. What we choose to do with this blessing is up to each one of us. I believe we should "pay it forward" to help another addict in need of guidance.

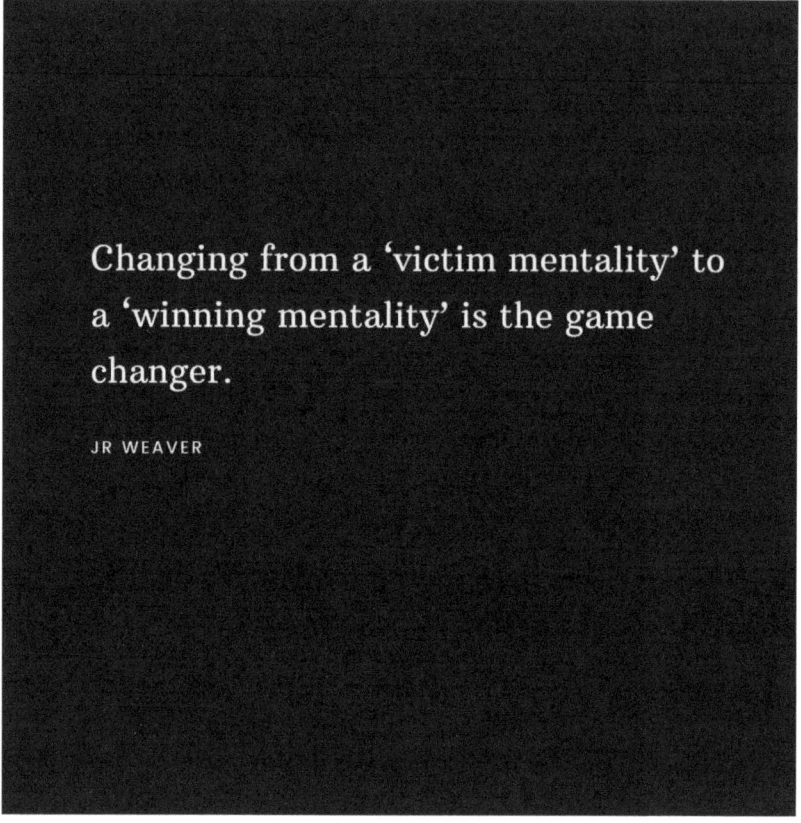

Changing Thoughts, Feelings, and Actions
Tired of the path that you're on? Nothing has worked, eh? Sobriety is more than not using or drinking. If we as addicts do not commit to changing ourselves, then we might as well expect to keep failing at recovery. A wise man recently told me that, if we fail to change our thought process, our feelings, and our actions, then we are not fully preparing ourselves for recovery. TFAs (Thoughts, Feelings, Actions) are about learning to reprogram our minds, taking yourselves off "autopilot," and relearning how to handle these situations

that often led to our relapsing. Each of us has the ability to analyze a situation and figure out the best potential outcomes. If you know that one drink leads to destruction then why drink that first one? If hanging out with "old friends" usually leads to using drugs, then why hang out with them?

Temptation will eventually win; we've all tried it, and we've probably all relapsed because of it. You have to be willing to change how your mind works. If situation A always leads to using, then common sense tells us to avoid situation A, right? How many times do we have to fall for the same pitfalls that lead us back to the exact situation that we so desperately wanted to escape?

> **ONE DAY YOU'RE GOING TO OPEN THAT DOOR TO THE PLACE THAT SCARES YOU AND REALIZE THAT ITS EMPTY INSIDE.**
>
> JR Weaver

I would like to believe that I am better than this, that each of us is better than this; we just have to know what addiction is planning and fortify ourselves against it by changing the way we are programmed. You're so much better than this addictive lifestyle; you just have to believe in yourself. Keep coming back! You're stronger than your addiction. It only win's when we completely surrender to it. One of the most difficult challenges you encounter will be how these new positive changes are perceived by your family and friends. Some may totally support the new, improved you, but some may still hold reservations based on the past. You can't expect others to automatically accept that you've changed. Why should they? How many times in the past have we said the same thing and fallen back into our addiction? They will need to see proof before jumping on the bandwagon, but do not lose faith or get discouraged. Any change is scary, even positive change, but stay on the path as if your future depends on it, because it does.

Stay focused and do not be afraid to seek help. People want to see you get better. I know it's difficult for anybody to take themselves out of their comfort zone and ask for help, but stay focused and do what you have to do to increase your chances at beating your demons. You may have distanced yourself from family during this time, and you will be pleasantly surprised that they may actually be your biggest supporters in recovery.

One of the first things you'll notice after being sober is that your life is improving. Relationships are slowly coming back, your self-esteem is rising, and you're starting to feel better mentally and physically. Sober me is way more social than my addict alter ego. During your active addiction, did you ever try to hold a conversation with another addict about real-world stuff? Outside of drugs, what else can you really talk about? We often misplace our loyalty to other addicts. Realistically, I wouldn't call them friends. How many times have they taken something of value from you? Money? Drugs? I was the same way when I hung out with other addicts; once the drugs ran out, I was out the door, looking for the next person to get me high. Once the addict takes a chemical into their system, the brain stops using common sense. It's strictly drugs, alcohol, and more drugs on the brain. Yes, our lives were completely centered around drugs; our addictions kept us captive! One of the biggest and hardest things is to take that first step. We are afraid to fail, and deep down inside, we may not fully want to be sober and accept life on life's terms. Most of us addicts will silently struggle on our own to get sober. Some may be able to just walk away cold turkey and never look back, but more often than not, without a strong support network we will find ourselves back in full blown addiction.

Be prepared to rebuild your social network in your early stages of recovery, maybe from the ground up! Isolating ourselves can be both good and bad, in my opinion. Sometimes being alone helps us deal with issues in our own time frame, but on the flip side, it can also be very dangerous to our recovery. It may lead to boredom and relapse. One of the things I used to navigate the early stages of my own recovery was social media, Facebook. I was fortunate to have a very supporting cyber family, and I really do appreciate what they have done for me. In our addiction, we often isolated ourselves from everyone, even other addicts at times. I know how it made me feel alone even when I was in a crowded room. That's the power of addiction on the mind; it wanted us to feel alone, even when we weren't.

Why? We were easier to control and manipulate into staying in our active addiction, no questions asked! I was a very social person before drugs took over my life. When I was using, I tended to be extremely introverted. It was a living hell. Part of me coveted being around other users, while the other part hated being around people. I couldn't be alone because that would make me start thinking I had a real problem, but I couldn't be around others either. It was a catch-22. Damned if I do and damned if I don't. Why do we isolate in our recovery too? Because we haven't learned to reprogram our thought process yet; we're afraid to go outside, so we stay inside and alone. This is dangerous for us in the early stages because we may start questioning this new sober lifestyle and if it's really worth it, since chances are we're bored and lonely. We have to learn how to have fun again, and that's a challenge for us because we know we are still in a vulnerable state. My advice is to make the extra effort at meeting new people that share common interests/goals. Arrive a few minutes earlier or stay a few minutes later but make the effort. The people at meetings want to help you, so chances are you will find yourself surrounded by people. If meetings aren't your thing, then try the gym. I think I read somewhere that exercising helps your recovery in a few ways. Read a book or go fishing. Try yoga, go to the movies, hang out with your family or sober friends, or go do the tourist thing and check out the scenic things. We have to make the effort to find new interesting things, whether family, AA, or church. We should have something to save us from relapsing. There is help out there, so my advice is to take advantage of it and give yourself a chance to win this fight against addiction. Just remember that your addiction doesn't want to lose control over you. It wants to keep you isolated and dependent on it.

Sober Today

One hour, one day at a time. Staying clean is a daily battle. We all know the path that relapsing will open: jails, institutions, and death. Screw that! Recovery opens doors that we had believed were closed permanently, such as reuniting with family and friends, happiness, employment, self-respect, etc. During my "down" years, I isolated myself from everyone, except other addicts. My thinking was that, if I hung out with addicts that were worse than me, then I must not have been that bad, right? Bullshit! I was only lying to myself, believing what my addiction wanted me to believe. That's what addiction wants. It has to keep you on a chain so you will continue to do its bidding. It wants to take you so far down the rabbit hole that you won't know which way leads back to the civilized world. I believe addicts will agree that addiction has pulled them from friends, family, and even children—and for what? We end up hating ourselves, and how do we cope? Self-medicating with more drugs and alcohol. Some of my fellow addicts may be just discovering this part of the addiction matrix. You're not alone. Your value has not diminished, and it's not too late to make amends, if you really want it. Deep down inside, I kept telling myself that I was so much better than this. *This* person wasn't really me, and you know what eventually happened? I started trying to recover on my own. Yes, I failed a few times, but I was trying. I finally started making better decisions, and then I made the best decision to put everything I had into recovery. I know I am still a long way from being done with my demons, but I am finally learning how to deal with life on life's terms, and I'm happy.

I just read a good post about "having time to do things," and it reminded me how we take time for granted. The truth is that we don't know if we do or don't. We can be in the best shape, physically, mentally, and spiritually, but none of that matters if it's your "time." Personally, I have so many things left that I want to do in this lifetime that it suddenly feels like I just don't have enough time left. But now I can pull my mind back to this moment and appreciate what I have accomplished so far on this journey. I'm proud of my sobriety and even prouder of my recovery. Most of you have watched me grow to the man I am today, and I'm not even close to the finished product. There is always something to improve, and every day, I get inspired to keep writing more and more. I was silent for a few months looking for that one shining moment that would fuel me to write these last twenty pages to wrap up this book, but I realized life isn't about "one glorious shining" moment. It's about all the little shining moments that feed our soul, that fuel our happiness, that help us become people.

Mindfulness and Addiction

- Promotes understanding and compassion rather than judgment and conflict with the addicted self.
- It allows the unconscious patterns to emerge to the conscious mind.
- It provides the opportunity for the rational mind to evaluate thoughts and dis-identify from them.
- It can create a window where the witness has the power to make a conscious decision.
- It has been used efficiently to break the cycle of addiction and compulsive behavior.

Recovery is a lifelong process, and it won't be easy. It will take a lifelong commitment from you, but seek and you shall find that life is beautiful when you finally break the chains of addiction. One of the most common mistakes in recovery is believing that you're cured when you stop using. Wrong! Being sober is much more than abstaining from drugs or alcohol. We must also strive to make life changes that will help prevent future relapse. We must change the way our minds think, the way we feel, and also the way we react to things. We simply cannot allow ourselves to continue to think, feel, or act the same way if we hope to change our lifestyles. How long do you think you can remain sober if you don't make these changes? If nothing changes, then *nothing changes*. If you don't make the change, then how can you expect anything else to change?

I had a discussion with a guy who has been clean for eight years. He was telling me that the only way to be a success story was to get some clean time under my belt, like him. I respectfully disagree. I think the main goal for each of us is to wake up sober each day. We all start our days with the same amount of clean time. Success is what happens each day in sobriety. That addiction of ours will always be there, patiently waiting on us to touch that first drop, trying to get us back on the path to our own destruction. Success is when a person stays sober today and wants a better way of life. Is my six-months recovery worth any less than his eight years? I think not. We can't rush the years of our recovery, but we can live each day sober, free from our disease.

Chris Hutcherson
Live in the moment. The past is irretrievable, and tomorrow never comes. Live in the moment. I blink, and the moment is over.

A Life Less Ordinary
Oh my God! What happened to us? Our life has become so bad, such a train wreck from abusing drugs and alcohol. Maybe we believed we could party for a few years and then stop to get on with our real life, but now it's

twenty years later, and we're homeless, broke, incarcerated, and addicted to drugs! That's how addiction takes over our lives. Fear not. There is hope, but it's never going to be easy. We know we can't touch drugs or alcohol ever again, but is that a bad thing? It's a good thing. Life begins again—family, friends, happiness. No more criminal activity, no more hiding from the police or waking up hating your life.

We would be lying to ourselves if we even started to think we could control addiction. Addiction wants you to believe that you might just be able to make things work out differently next time. BS! I have a long history of relapsing and incarcerations to testify to that. Will the cravings or thoughts about drugs ever stop? I don't know. Probably not for a long time if you're fortunate. I still have the random drug dream or thought about using, but I'm learning to push the temptations aside because I accept that it's ludicrous to entertain any thoughts about using.

All I know is that I am sober today. Hopefully, you're sober too. We must help each other, one day at a time. The path to recovery is a treacherous path with relapse only a minute away, waiting, wanting, whispering to each of us, pushing us to just that "one drink or one hit," but we know what that one hit or drink starts, and it's not worth it. We have to be mentally stronger each day to beat addiction. Make the effort to get back your life back. I know I am. Stand up to your addiction. It's a good thing. It's not losing to relapse because you're making the effort to get better. Just keep on plugging away, and hopefully it sticks next time.

Trust the process. Tweak it along the way so that it works best for you. If attending meetings keeps you sober today, then keep going. Find new positive friends who want the same good things that you do and start rebuilding your life. We are no longer in denial, so we know what's good or bad for us. What we do from this point forward will determine where we go from here. You got this! Alone, I am just one addict trying to live each day sober. I have no illusions of who I am anymore or where I have been or what I have done, all at the bidding of my addiction. I know I have lived the miserable life of a hardcore drug addict, staying in hotels, sleeping in cars or on couches or floors. Why? Because I let my addiction control me. It told me that only drugs mattered. The addiction matrix had me, bought and paid for. It took everything I had...cars, family, friends. And what did it give in return? Misery. Anger. It took everything I had to break the spell of addiction, but finally, after being blinded and misled for over twenty years by addiction, I finally admitted that I couldn't do "this" anymore. I needed help, professional and spiritual. I sought help from the VA, drug court, and my higher power.

I am humbled to say that my future is looking better every day because I am sober and no longer in active addiction. Do not give up the fight; never give up. I believe all addicts begin the recovery process during their active addiction. It could be the random thought about not using today or about thinking how to get their life back. Mine began when I questioned what I was doing with my life. Was I truly going to let my addiction control my future? Deep down, I knew I was better than what I had become. I tried sobering up on my own and managed to string together some dry time before eventually relapsing. I tried controlling my usage, but that never lasted either. I learned that addicts like myself cannot beat addiction alone. We have to accept that fact and ask for help. If we truly want to get better, we have to take ourselves out of our comfort zone. I was fortunate to be a military vet, so I had the VA to help. I took myself out of my comfort zone and admitted to the VA that I had a severe substance-abuse problem.

I wanted to get better and committed myself to their rehab program, which included a personal case manager (Lauren Nelson) and a psychiatrist (Dr. Braxton). Most addicts will admit that, in the beginning, we are not entirely comfortable talking about our dark days. Who wants to admit we lost control of our lives? Well, if you were crazy enough to do whatever to get high, then shouldn't you give the same effort to get better? And yes, in the beginning, I wasn't truly open and honest. I didn't give the program 100 percent. I only did what was needed to graduate.

I finished rehab, and guess what happened? I relapsed again. I went on a binge that lasted a few months. I wasn't planning on relapsing—or maybe subconsciously I was. Relapse happens when you start skipping out on what kept you sober. It could take weeks to actually use, but the seed may have been planted months prior. My addiction waited patiently for me to graduate rehab and played to my ego, telling me how strong I now was and how I could control my drug use. I bought into that, hook, line, and sinker! That's what addiction does to us. We have to accept that we cannot control ourselves once drugs or alcohol enters our system. We've tried dozens of times and always failed. Accept it and get better. It's all or nothing with us. We're addicts for life. We have to be able to spot the early warning signs, like thoughts of using, irritability, loss of appetite or sleep, skipping meetings. Then we must take immediate action. Call a sober friend, talk to your sponsor, or catch a meeting—whatever! We have to commit ourselves to whatever helped us sober up. We all want to be sober, but we need to keep constantly reminding ourselves that, if we do drugs, we lose everything that we worked so hard to get back.

1. **Precontemplation**: We do not believe that we have a problem or that we need help.

2. **Contemplation**: We start to accept that we do have a problem and start considering how we can make a change.

3. **Action**: We start taking steps toward our recovery. We do the meetings or classes; we change our lifestyle and our thought patterns.

4. **Maintenance**: We are working a recovery program that helps us stay clean. We continue to avoid the negative things, such as people, places, and things that could trigger us. We limit our exposure to anything that doesn't help us move forward.

How did we become stone-cold addicts? I'm pretty sure my high school guidance counselor would say that wasn't on my list of goals. If you are like me, then you probably started out socially drinking or smoking weed. Everything was kosher in the beginning, right? We had things under control. We were still motivated to conquer the world. We were young and had that youthful swag; we were invincible, right? That's the addiction trap—letting us believe that *everything is ok* and that we're just using for fun and can stop whenever. Slowly, that social using starts becoming more and more routine. Then one day, we wake up a few months or years later, and—boom!—our first thought of the day is how can we get high. We don't care about anything else. Hell, we couldn't even think about anything else until we got that first one in us to make us feel "normal."

That was our addictive mindset keeping us under control. It knew that, once that drink or drug hit our system, we would become slaves to our addictions. Now that you have some sober time under your belt and the fog is starting to clear from your mind, you can see the sometimes-slow (sometimes-fast) evolution of how addiction tricked you into becoming what you are today. Addiction is sneaky like that. It doesn't mind letting you think you're in control in the beginning because it knows, sooner or later, you will belong to it. It will spoon-feed us until it knows it has us in its grip, and then it will start the isolation process. We will have to decide at some point to give up what we know for the false promises of addiction. This is where many of us give up on our goals under the pretense that we will come back to them later. Unfortunately, later never comes back for some of us. Work? Addiction will let us work to keep that paycheck coming in until our work starts getting in the way of getting high. Then we usually don't show up for our next shift, or we get fired. But we'll get back another job, it tells us, eventually. School? Sure, it will let us think we can do school and drugs for now. Eventually, we start skipping class and end up failing or dropping out. But then we have our addiction telling us we can go back, eventually. Family? Sure, we can hang out with our families. Who better to manipulate for money? Until our families tell us to get lost. Again we're told that we can get them back, eventually. The list goes on and on, and do you think it's going to let us cash in on those promises? Not today, but eventually, sometime farther down the road. It's crazy the things we believe in our active addiction. It makes us not care about anything but getting high and maintaining that high. Everything we do revolves around feeding it. I want to tell you that you don't have to live like that. Do not believe what addiction is telling you about not having a chance for a normal life. That's complete BS. I have been doing these NA celebration meetings at the VA on Friday nights, and I am telling you that these people are living their life free from drugs or alcohol. They are happy, joyous, and free. And you can get that too. You have to want it; that's all. You have to want a better way of life. You are never so far gone that you can't come back. You don't have to live like that anymore. No more just one more! I can show you how, but you have to want this more than anything. You're fighting against something that doesn't want to let you go. It may have owned you, but it's so very possible to get out from under its control. Come on. Say it with me: No more just one more! Free yourself and live the life you were blessed with.

RELAPSE AND RELAPSE PREVENTION

So your attempts at staying sober keep failing? Why keep torturing yourself, only to fail yet again? You're starting to believe that you're different and that you can't beat this addiction? BS! You need to change your attitude right now. Believe it or not, each time you attempt to get sober, you are gaining strength. Whether you make it a day or three months, you're stronger, and those chains of addiction are getting weaker. Your mind and body are getting stronger. Your addiction wants you to believe that you can't win, but it's scared; it senses that you're changing, you're building up your defenses, and you're so damn close to turning your life around.

Do not give up! You're so much stronger than you may believe. You've got this!

Have you realized that your true friends and family want you to succeed? They want sober you making the decisions in your life. They are willing to help, but you need to show them a true effort, that you're serious this time about recovery. Freedom from chasing that addiction—it will be one of the best decisions, the best feeling when you finally start breaking away from the addiction matrix and start getting your life back on track.

I was out there on the streets, alone, miserable. Hanging with people that I really didn't care about—but misery loves company. I was lost in the addiction matrix. It blinded me to the reality that I was throwing away my life. My life! Do you see now what it's doing to you? Screw that! I want to be happy. I want to be loved. Drugs are the fast track to none of that. Your addiction wants your soul. It turns you away from everything in your life that was good. How many of you have left your family and friends behind? Your children? When you start to sober up, do you miss them? What do you do then? You self-medicate to forget; that's what addiction wants you to do. It's a vicious cycle, with the answer always being more drugs, despite drugs being the reason for your problems. That's the matrix!

We may be powerless over our addiction, but we are powerful over our recovery. I tested myself last year, and how do you think it worked out? Not well. I was cruising along in my sobriety and had stacked up about 4 months of clean time. I thought I was stronger this time around, that one hit wouldn't hurt, right? I was working two jobs and had just graduated from rehab gotten a new place to live. Well, the first night, I wanted to test myself, so I called an old dealer and picked something up. Before the night was over, I had called the old dealer a few more times and spent a few hundred dollars. That's not the worst of it. I ended up losing one of my jobs because I didn't show up, didn't call in to let them know either. Addiction told me I was ok since I had another job, right?

Well, I started stealing from my other job to fuel my binge. Eventually, I got fired when the inventory started to get out of whack. The sad thing is, I really liked the job. After I was terminated from that job, my addiction told me to sneak back to get more items to trade for drugs. But I was unaware that the owner had installed a new camera system, which of course, caught me stealing. I was eventually charged with burglary. That's what addiction does. Four felonies to score just a little bit of drugs and lose a great job. I could have dwelled on it and totally lost myself to addiction to forget about it all, but I did something unexpected. I started to get sober. I started down the path of recovery, and believe it or not, I got my original job back. Life is strange, but what they say about recovery and things turning around really is true. When you're sick and tired of being sick and tired, then you know you're truly ready to take the action needed to get your life back.

Stress is one of the main reasons we relapse, possibly number one on the list. Work or family stress, life in general—it all adds up to relapse if we do not learn how to relax and deal with whatever issues are causing it. Guilt is the remorse for something you may have done. Shame is the feeling you have inside for doing something. When you start feeling overwhelmed, check yourself. Life isn't easy, and you should expect a few bumps in the road, but stay focused and remember that recovery is not easy. There are days when it feels like the weight of the world is on your shoulders. You just want to numb out to everyone and everything. You can't expect your addiction to ever release the pressure to use. You should expect to be tested early and often. I'm here to testify that it does get easier. The longer you stay clean, the better you will feel. The addiction fog that clouded your thinking is starting to lift, and you can finally see the light. You learn to appreciate life and the things that make life beautiful. We had to humble ourselves to get to this amazing opportunity to live again.

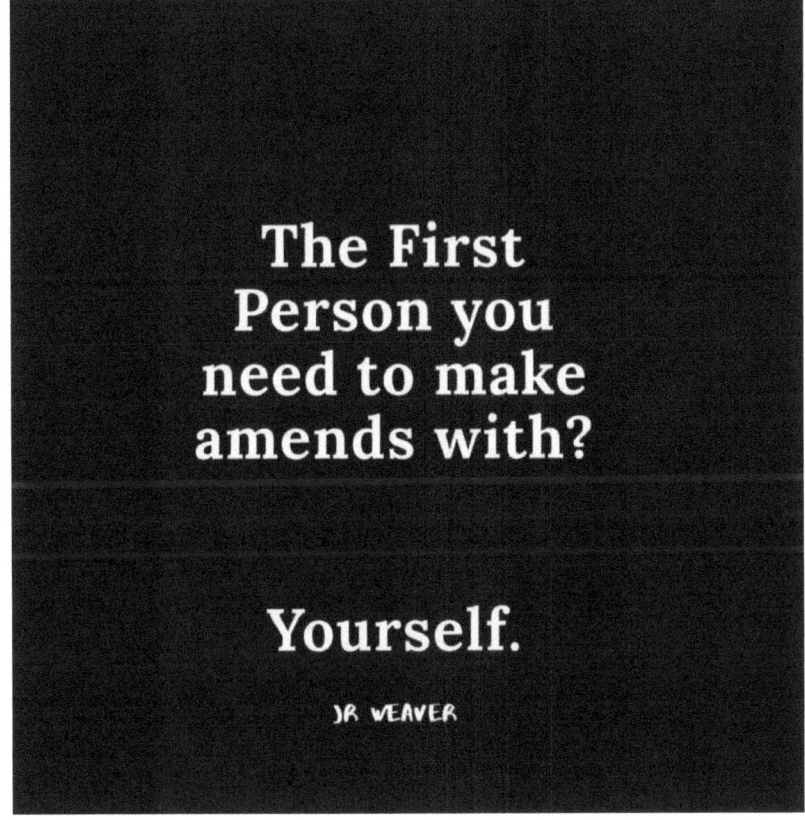

We went *full blast* into our addiction, so we need to bring that same effort to our recovery. I walk a mile to catch two buses to get to work Monday through Friday. I have long days with evening classes on Monday, Tuesday, and Thursday. I leave my house by 5:30 a.m., and I don't get home until after 9:00 p.m., but to me, it's totally worth every minute. I would rather sober up out here on the outside rather than on the inside locked up.

If I can make it out here today, then that builds up my strength to resist my demons down the road. My demons have owned me for over twenty years. Yes, they let me have brief stints of sobriety because they knew I wasn't ready to stop. You have to be ready to stop using *all drugs.* Do not BS yourself and think you can switch to another drug or continue drinking. You have to admit that you have a problem. We can't control it, and we've tried and failed, countless times. It just doesn't work. Do not for a minute think that you're different, that you're going to be the one addict in the history of addicts who can make the switch and live happily ever after. It doesn't work that way. Thousands have tried, and thousands have fallen prey to their drugs of choice before long.

And we don't get to start over. We start right back at the point of where we left off. Addiction might even want "more" from you this next time. What do you think your addiction is doing right now? Do you think it's just sitting there on the sidelines, patiently waiting for another opportunity? Well, yes, but it's also in the gym, working out, getting bigger, badder, and stronger. It's watching the game tapes of your life, trying to find a weakness to exploit. This game is serious. Your life is on the line, so I can only pray that you take this seriously. I know a few of you will be thinking, "Yeah, he has a good point, but I'm not really ready to give up the life."

What life are you referring to? The life of spending every penny for drugs or drinks? The life of being alone and not being part of your family? The life of waiting in the crappiest of motels for some shady drug dealer to short you on some wack drugs? These dealers are not your friends; you're a business transaction. They aren't there to bless you with weight or quality. Yeah, they may sit around and "hang out" with you. But wake up; they are only there for more of your money. What happens when you spend your last dollar and ask for a small credit? See ya! This life? That's what you want?

Really? How about the times you woke up the day *after* payday, broke, no smokes, no gas, no food? We always forget about the hard times, but chances are you're thinking about them now, eh? Our addiction doesn't want us to remember the bad times. It knows you would be repulsed. You have a chance to turn things around right *now*. When was the last time you treated yourself to something nice? A nice steak dinner or a new pair of shoes? A nice night out with the family or kids? Think about what's possible, compared to what's happening right now.

Just for Today
I no longer regret my past because. With it, I can share with other addicts, perhaps averting the pain—or even death—of another.

ADDICTION MATRIX

Welcome to your life, a once promising life full of potential. Do you remember the days when friends and family were actually happy to see you? What happened? You know exactly what happened; addiction happened. You thought you could control it, that you were in control of everything. You just got played by the addiction matrix! But we all do sooner or later. Are you now understanding what happened to you and your once-great life? What would you give to get it all back? Your family, your friends, your children? Don't play yourself, thinking you can be in control of your addiction. You can't. Accept it. You must accept it and respect the power of addiction; it plays for keeps.

    Think back to all the time you spent chasing that high, the money you wasted, the personal relationships and jobs you may have lost. Remember all of it and let the anger and regret over all of it sink in for a minute. Now use that! Next time that addiction wants to start whispering in your ear just remember what it has promised you in the past and what it actually cost you. Would you let somebody use and abuse you over and over? I hope not. I hope you can learn and be smart enough to say no the next time. You have the power to stop being addicted, no matter what. You just have to want more out of life. Do you? If given a choice, would you stop using drugs and get your life back or continue using drugs and destroy your life? Which do you think most active addicts would choose? During my active addiction, sadly I would choose option 2. Addiction is a powerful manipulator; it will control you beyond reason. It will diminish everything, except getting high. It will tear you away from friends and family without a second thought. It will turn your life upside down until you lose everything. Then it will wait patiently while you try to build yourself back up then slap you again!

Addiction will go full savage on your once-normal life and reduce you to living on the streets, alone and desperate.

What makes a select few people go from normal users to full-blown addicts? Genes? DNA? Our minds? How does a guy like me go from abusing alcohol to abusing drugs? Can I blame my PTSD or my depression or anxiety or not being hugged enough as child? I could, but I won't. I don't know why I flipped from normal guy to super-addict guy. Addiction is hard to explain to someone who has no experience being controlled by something. Our minds crave escape, and the only way to escape is to use drugs or alcohol. I continued to feed myself half truths about my problems to rationalize my addiction.

It's one of life's true mysteries how a substance can control your mind and take over your life, even if you're aware that it's leading you down a self-destructive path. The addiction matrix slowly takes over your mind to the point that you once could have held food, clothing, shelter, and drugs in equal value—but now your mind is dominated by drugs, drugs, and more drugs. Addiction doesn't care how or what you have to do to get drugs either. Pay your rent or bills? Not today. It's drugs, and screw everything and everyone else. What if you're broke and can't afford any drugs? Addiction tells you to do whatever it takes to get to that next high. Legal or illegal, it's all fair in this war going through your mind. If you happen to get arrested while in pursuit of drugs? Don't worry. Addiction will be waiting for you when you get out of jail. It will always be there, waiting to tempt you back into its cold embrace. It's a serious disease, and each user must decide sooner or later which path to follow: addiction or sobriety.

> ## Mindfulness-based Relapse Prevention
>
> *become aware of personal triggers and automatic reactions
> *learn to pause, think, and notice before reacting to situations
> *cultivate a new relationship with perceived discomforts to avoid masking it
> *allow for non-judgmental compassion for yourself and your life experiences
> *create a mindful lifestyle to support full physical, mental, and emotional health

Addicts cannot be recreational users. Our brains and bodies are wired differently than normal people's. Eventually, we cannot continue to deny that we have a problem. I had a choice to make: continue using and destroy myself in the process or put in the work toward recovery and reclaim my life. It wasn't easy to stop using. It never will be. But the rewards will make your life so much better. I have been through rehab, through drug classes, and I'm just wired differently than others.

My first positive step was admitting I was a true addict. I accepted that I could not control myself, and I sought help. It was a gradual process in the beginning, and I was scared beyond anything in this world that I would fail again. I stopped using and started avoiding situations that always led to relapse. I avoided people, places, and things that I'd once associated with drugs, and I finally started to break those chains of addiction. If you want to save your life, then you must make the effort to change. You have reached the point in your life where you're just tired, like I was. Life is so much more than chasing the next high. Open your eyes and heart to the beauty that is life, and you will never regret it. I know I am glad I finally did.

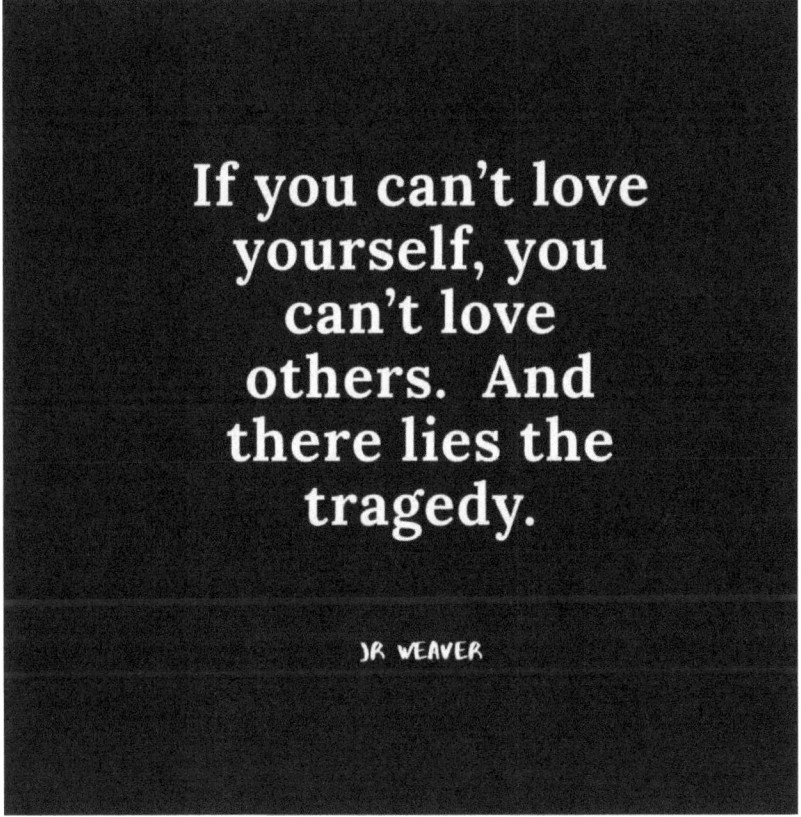

Ok, so you're living a life of addiction because it's your life and you can do whatever you want, right? You think you're only hurting yourself, and you might even believe you can stop whenever you want. When addiction is in control of you, it only allows you to think about...guess what? Addiction. We believe that we control our life and that what we do to our families or friends is only collateral damage. We don't think we're hurting anybody else, but the reality is that we are hurting all those that loved us. I never noticed what I was doing to anybody in pursuit of my next hit. My mind was focused on getting high, and my addiction wouldn't let me think of anything else. Why do you think that was? Addiction knows that, once we start questioning things, once we start noticing the damage it has done to our life, we will finally have to look in the mirror and admit to ourselves that we have a major problem. If we don't do something about it now, then we will destroy any chances of a normal life.

During my active addiction, I only cared about getting high and feeding my addiction. I started to hate myself and tried to justify my growing drug habit. How can we tell ourselves anything else? We actually lie to ourselves to keep us from looking at ourselves. I believe addiction takes us to that make-or-break point in our lives. We either keep running with it until we're dead or arrested—or we ask for help. I call that Basic Addiction 101—doing anything and everything to satisfy that overwhelming addictive urge. You are living only for your addiction.

I knew men and women on the street who walked away from their children. From their children! That's how powerful this addiction thing can be. I talked to guys in my cell block that couldn't wait to get out to get high again. Addiction has a way of blocking out all the bad things in our brains so we don't always register that it was our addiction that got us arrested! Inmates will talk about how they have been incarcerated for months, waiting to go to trial, calling their families every day, telling them how they are done with the drugs and alcohol.

I was the exact same way, and my sobriety quickly ended the minute I was released. Except this last time, I know what it was that got me in trouble, and I refuse to give it power over me ever again. The reality of sobriety may intimidate you, but fear not. It gets easier each day. How can you face real life without any mind-altering substances? One day at a time. You will do it for yourself, and you will do it for your family, your children. They miss the real you. The past can be forgotten, and your future hasn't been written yet. It's time for you to come back home.

> You're a warrior, warriors don't give up and they don't back down. Pick up your sword and shield and fight.

Sober Strong!

Today, I will live my life according to what's best for *me*! I will not let drugs or alcohol control my life. I have learned through recovery that I am just like the other addicts, and do you know what? It doesn't bother me for a minute. I think we had to fall hard to figure out what we wanted in life. I know for a fact that my addiction took from me whatever it wanted, and I have a long road of recovery in front of me. I know I will catch some criticism for being open and honest about my past, and I really don't care, but what I do care about is today. I woke up sober *today*, and I am truly at peace with myself. That is a long way from where my addiction had me just last year. Addiction is a manipulator; it will say anything to get you or me to take that first hit or first drink. It knows that, once that chemical enters our bodies, we will be doomed to repeat the vicious cycle again. We have to stay strong and active in our recovery if we want to avoid falling back to becoming slaves to our addiction.

How do we stay sober strong? We do whatever we have to do. We go to any lengths to stay sober. We go to AA/NA meetings, SMART Recovery meetings, church, the beach. We spend time with our families, we read books, and we go to the movies. We avoid anybody who doesn't support our recovery, and we work to get our self-esteem and self-confidence back on track. We do things that make us feel better about ourselves.

I joined Planet Fitness last week. Working out helps me feel better about myself. I call this my recovery workout session. Getting back in shape is a blessing to me. Working out is something that I have really enjoyed doing over the years, and I am happy to be able to enjoy it again. It builds your confidence, and you feel so much better.

I hit a Reiki class and totally felt de-stressed when I left. (Reiki is a Japanese technique for stress reduction that also promotes healing). Recovery yoga? Why not? Recovery yoga combines twelve steps and yoga. It promotes recovery from the substances or thinking that hold you back from enjoying the freedom you seek. I say find what works best for you and can keep you motivated in your recovery. That's what will keep you sober today, and that, my friends, is one more day free from the drugs, alcohol, and your addiction.

TMS for addiction? Transcranial magnetic stimulation was originally researched for helping with depression (yes, I have done this for depression with positive results), but now they think it may help with substance abuse (and yes, I have tried it for this too with positive results). The patient is seated in a chair with the coils in a headpiece that will send magnetic pulses to the brain. The technical description goes something like this: Electromagnetic coils that create a magnetic field on the prefrontal cortex hit the nerve cells in the brain. The belief is that these repetitive electrical currents will work in the deep recesses of the brain by stimulating the neurons that are tied to mood and restore them to normal functioning. I remember signing up for the research study with skepticism, but about halfway through the study, I noticed a big change in my reactions to certain drug memories that I had to think about while being strapped to the chair. I remember telling Sarah that my drug using thoughts were having less of an effect on me.

Today, I took in my very first SMART Recovery (Self-Management and Recovery Training) class, and I really liked it. It's similar to AA/NA, without the spirituality side. SMART teaches that you aren't powerless against your addictions, and you can recover. If you've tried the AA/NA way and it wasn't your flavor, then I highly recommend checking this out. The people were great. We shared our stories and talked about life today. I will definitely be back every Saturday at 1:00 p.m. For more information, check out www.smartrecovery.org for meeting times and locations. I believe that there is no "one program that fits all," and we all owe it to our own recovery to keep building up our defenses to stay ahead of our addictions.

SMART Recovery Four Main Points

Four-Point Program

1. **Motivation to Abstain** - Enhancing and maintaining motivation to abstain from addictive behavior
2. **Coping with Urges** - Learning how to cope with urges and cravings
3. **Problem Solving** - Using rational ways to manage thoughts, feelings and behaviors
4. **Lifestyle Balance** – Balancing short-term and long-term pleasures and satisfactions in life

The following information is the blueprint to how we became addicted to drugs and/or alcohol. It's a vicious cycle for us because our minds react differently than regular people's. Now that we can identify how it started, we can figure out where each of us is currently at in the process and plan accordingly.

THE CYCLES OF ADDICTION

- *Drinking or Using Drugs*
  Active addiction. We're using without caring about anything or anyone.

- *Control or Bargaining*
  We figure out we have a problem. Our first instinct is to control or cut down on our usage. We might try only using on weekends or using less. We've all been here, tried, and failed. You can't control addiction for any length of time, and soon you're right back to using daily.

- *Abstinence from Using Drugs or Alcohol*
  We try to stop everything. We have the best intentions of stopping, but addiction has a way of sticking around. We may stop for a few weeks to prove to ourselves that we're capable of stopping and then use again to justify returning. That's our addiction misleading us back. We were never in control, and addiction let us believe that because it knew it could manipulate us back if we thought we could stop whenever we wanted. The truth is that we can't stop for long by ourselves.

- *Stop Using but Not Changing Your Life*
  We finally manage to string along some clean time, but we don't make any changes in the way we live. We still want to hang out with our addicted friends in the same areas. Again, our addiction is playing us. It

knows that, sooner or later, we will pick up and be right back where we were.

- *Total Abstinence with a Life Change*
We finally start seeing the light. We know we can't go on living this way. We tried to stop on our own, we tried to control our usage, we tried to stop without making any life changes, and none of it has worked. Now we are faced with the reality that this isn't going to be easy. We have to stop using altogether. We have to make life changes. We are going to have to adopt some type of recovery program if we want any chance at a normal life. Nervous? Don't worry; it will get easier, and life will get better faster than you believe. People want to see you beat your addiction. Take it one day at a time. Keep yourself busy doing productive things and don't forget to enjoy some "me" time to recharge your batteries. I have been clean about six months, and I am enjoying my life. Life is beautiful; it isn't always easy, but you will discover the good times. The precious moments that you will cherish for the rest of your life are so much better than sitting around paranoid, alone and miserable. Choose life.

Knowing what to Expect

Relapse is the process of returning to drugs or alcohol after a period of abstinence.

We have to stay alert to the clues that our addictions are making another attempt to bring us back. Clues can be anything that change our behavior, attitudes, feelings, thoughts, or a mix of all of these. Knowing when you need to be more proactive in your recovery can help you before any potential relapse.

Behavior—can be explained as anything that changes our moods or emotions. It can be a quick temper with others, or maybe we stop doing what helped us get and stay sober, recovery work like meetings, or maybe we're just at out risky behaviors like hanging out in bad places, increased stress.

Attitudes—When you start questioning the sobriety lifestyle, maybe you're wondering if it's worth it. Or maybe you are debating about your life's direction in general. During our addiction, we generally kept a negative attitude; it helped us accept the bad things we had to do to maintain our drug usage.

Thoughts—Dangerous thoughts about "rewarding ourselves" or "deserving" a night of using drugs or alcohol to celebrate something. Thinking it couldn't hurt or maybe we are starting to think that nobody would know. Maybe we believe that we're cured now and have found the secret to controlling our demons. Our addiction is hoping we forget that we can't do just one hit or one drink; we must always remember that, once we allow ourselves to put that drug into our body, we are doomed. We are going to go into full-blown relapse, and everything that we built up will be gone before our binge is finished. We don't do just one hit or one drink; we do many. We have tried time and time again to control our usage, and what happened each time? We lost, and we lost bad.

Feelings—Feelings can be anything—an increase in moodiness, depression, boredom, or being angry. A common relapse issue can be attributed to ending a personal relationship or maybe a rocky relationship. It's human nature to be upset or angry at our partner for whatever.

We have to be aware of these clues and be ready to deal with them before they build up. Always remember that our addictions are out there waiting for us, they don't sleep. This is where having our relapse prevention plan ready will save you.

Positive Thinking

Staying positive during recovery is mandatory. Surround yourself with a positive support group that will help you navigate the daily addiction minefield and keep you sober. Positive reinforcement keeps the addict proactive and motivated to stay sober. Recovery isn't a three-day program that will cure you at the end; it's a daily maintenance plan to help keep the addict from relapsing and falling back into the addict lifestyle. Addiction will always be there, waiting to invade your inner thoughts, but your recovery plan is designed to deal with these attacks before they can get a foothold on your recovery and reprogram your brain into the good-versus-bad mental debate of that first hit or drink. If a user reaches this stage, then we should have positive support that will help us through the moment. Go to a meeting. Being around other recovering addicts that are battling their own demons is a safe and positive environment that will help keep you sober.

Go fishing or bowling; go work out. Positive activities will make you feel good and on the right path and also keep you motivated. Just take it one day at a time. During my addiction years, I would like to believe that I didn't change that much, but I would be in denial. The addiction mindset believes the small changes we accept don't affect others, that others expect addicts to act a certain way, so we accept these small changes in behavior. The overall damage that we are doing to our personal relationships is insane; we're betraying and destroying them slowly. Addicts may actually believe what they are saying to friends and families—that's the sad truth. But when that drug or drink enters our system, it's off to the races! All bets are off, and we're on a binge that takes no prisoners. It's manipulative in its simplest form; addiction wants drugs, and we do whatever it takes to satisfy that hunger. Our best chance, our only chance, is sobriety and recovery. That's real talk.

Most of us addicts can remember sitting in jail, waiting for a court date or release date so we can get back out on the streets and continue getting high. I was one of them. I have stacked such a huge arrest record, all in the pursuit of getting high. I could be angry with myself, but I'm not. I have started on a sober path, and finally my head and heart are in a good place. I know it won't be easy; addiction will never give up its attempt to bring me back, but I know what I want out of my life, and there is no place for addiction in it. To allow myself that one hit or drink that will destroy everything that I worked so hard on is unacceptable to me. I have discovered a motivation to clean up my life, and it all begins when I wake up sober.

Today, my color was called for drug screening, and since it's Saturday, they have abbreviated hours, so I had to rush to catch two buses to make it in time. I have no fear of testing positive, since I've been sober for over five months now. Testing negative for drugs is a tiny victory for me. I'm rewarded with the knowledge that I am sober and on the right track to getting my life back. I decided to take the next bus to the Otranto Library so I could write a little bit about my life. Currently, my life is a struggle; it's not easy by any means, but I did not expect any miracles to happen immediately. Check this out: life isn't meant to be easy, but compared to the days when I was using each and every day, life is a blessing.

    I have noticed former addicts, myself included, talking about the days and nights of getting high and the struggles that they had to endure to get money or find drugs to escape from the reality that was "our" life. The common misconception about these so-called "war stories" is that it was fun and easy. The truth of the matter is that it wasn't. The drugs and money required didn't just miraculously appear each time; you had to do some work to get your supplies, and unfortunately most of us didn't have fat bank accounts to get a never-ending supply of drugs. You had a major substance addiction, and you had to feed it because it was all you could think about. Most of the time, we would run out of money and be forced to do illegal or idiotic things to satisfy our cravings. I boosted (stole) things from stores and people, I drove dealers and escorts around, I fenced stolen merchandise from other addicts, I wrote fraudulent checks or did phony deposits to banks, and I stole money from family members because I was deep in my addiction, and it made me believe that it was all part of the game, and part of me believed that whatever I pawned or borrowed I would get back from the pawn stores or whatever. I never did. I lost laptops, tools, jewelry. My addiction told me it was ok to lose everything, so why bother spending money to get my stuff back when I could spend any money on my next high? Lying, cheating, and stealing were things that we accepted during our addiction. I can honestly say that my past is something I would love to do over, but it's not possible. I can make amends today by staying sober and living a life that isn't controlled by any substances. I wasted twenty years chasing a "feeling" created by illegal substances—for what? To "escape" from my reality that life wasn't good? I had a good life before I started using. Yeah, I had problems, but we all do. One of my goals for this book is to keep myself sober by writing about the experiences that I went through during my addiction and to explain the thought patterns that goes through our minds that somehow justified what we did to ourselves to feed our addictions. I hope to reach out to the still-struggling addicts and let them know they still have options to take back control of their lives. I once believed I was "stuck" living that life, that the only way out of it was death or incarceration. Believing that was ridiculous, and it led me to almost ruining my life.

I wish I didn't have to go through what I did to realize that there is more to life than drugs, but now I realize I have the opportunity and platform to share my story with the masses and hopefully help someone find the path to escape that life. I know I have a long way to go to prove myself, and I can accept that reality as long as I prove to my biggest critic, myself, that I can do this. I will always be a few quick minutes away from relapse, and guess who will always be there waiting for me to screw up? Addiction! The truth is that it will wait patiently in the back of your mind; it will know when you're weakest and hit you with a barrage of thoughts about using, and it will paint the prettiest picture in the world to lure you back. We have to remember all the BS that goes with it to keep it from regaining a foothold in our minds. If I have to work twice as hard to get to work, if I have to walk in the rain or take four bus rides Monday through Friday to get to work and drug classes or meetings, then that's exactly what I will do. We can't deny that we did crazier things to get drugs, so why should sobering up be easy? It is getting easier to do whatever it takes to make it through my day sober, so I trust the process. The drug dreams eventually start going away, and the thoughts of using slowly go away with time too. One of my counselors used the analogy of "starving the cat," which basically explains that, if you don't feed a stray cat, it will eventually go away. If we don't feed our addiction, then it will come around less and less. (Credit to John Palmer for this illustration). By staying sober, we will eventually disarm addictive thoughts, and I believe that it does get easier.

Experts typically agree that the first thirty days are usually the toughest. I would like to extend that out even farther to a full six months. My reasoning is that it takes every addict about that long to develop new habits, good, clean, productive habits. We are learning to reprogram our minds, our actions, our thoughts. All of this is needed to help break the addiction cycle and risk of relapsing. We will never be fully cured, and we have to live with

that knowledge each and every day. We have to want to wake up sober and find the moments in each day that bring us joy
. And believing that our lives are so much better and meaningful without the use of any foreign substance. Keeping the mind on point is a difficult task; we all should be aware the mind has a habit of drifting off if we allow it to go unchecked. Drugs and alcohol will always be just a thought away, with relapse only a moment away, if we allow it. We can't erase these thoughts, but we can learn to reprogram new sober thoughts to replace these older, constant-user thoughts. Exercise the mind!

Once upon a time, I was an avid reader. I enjoyed it—the escape or challenge to learning something new. Addiction took that away from me. I couldn't focus long enough to get into a book anymore. I had to relearn how to focus my mind to stay focused on reading, and guess what? I started to read again! I refuse to let addiction control me or any other parts of my life. I've read more books in the last thirty days than I have in the last twenty years. It is possible to regain interest in old hobbies and recreational activities, if you put in the effort. One of my goals today is trying to be a better person each day; it's difficult because other people and events don't always cooperate, but I've learned to avoid dangerous or unpleasant situations, if possible. Living life on life's terms! Just for today, I will examine the level of honesty in my life.

> 'Cause at the end of the day you gotta decide for yourself. Those demons promise you it'll be different next time, and thats possible 'cause you might not make it back.
>
> JR WEAVER

Helping Others Stay Sober

How can we help others if we can barely help ourselves? Helping others will actually help you stay sober. We should always make sure that we are in a good place in our own recovery before attempting to help others. Helping another person is a rewarding feeling that will help us stay sober and on the right path. AA principles are built on sharing with another addict, but the other person has to really want recovery. You can't rush someone because you could turn them against the process if you're overzealous. Let them ask about recovery and be ready to share your own story. They should see how similar your own story is to theirs, and then hopefully, they may open up to the thought of sobering up.

One of the best things is watching the "change" happen in another addict, when they finally and totally accept recovery and are willing to go to any lengths to keep sober. I can look back at my past mistakes and wonder what I was thinking. I almost ruined a chance at a great life. I was blinded to the damage that I was inflicting on myself and others. Addiction played me like a first-class chump, and I can accept that I lost badly. When we start to understand addiction and how cunning and diabolical it can be, we can start planning a solid recovery foundation. Addiction doesn't want to lose its foothold, so don't think it will quietly fade into the background. It will always be there, waiting, plotting. Believe in yourself and believe that you can stay sober; that is what changes the game.

Addiction only wins when we surrender completely! Do not let it win! Never give up! This is your life! The hardest step to recovery is the very first step. We were blinded by our addiction, to the extent of our rapidly decaying life. Now we know what addiction wants from us, so what are *you* going to do about that? Today, I will do the work that my recovery needs. Our recovery should always be in our thoughts; do not think that you are good after a few months of sobriety. It doesn't work like that. That is exactly what our addiction wants us to do. Never underestimate the power of addiction. It will always be there, plotting another relapse. It probably has already picked a time and a place. It can be weeks or months from now. It only takes a moment of insanity for relapse to strike down the strongest of us. Remember that. It takes only a few minutes to erase all the beautiful things that your recovery made possible.

Recovery is not easy. There are days when it feels like the weight of the world is on your shoulders. Your sobriety will be tested early and often. Keep believing that things will get better because I am here to testify that they do! The longer you're able to stay clean, the better you will feel. That addiction "fog" that clouded our thinking will be lifted. We will finally be able to see the things that our addiction didn't want us to see. You will be amazed that you were blinded for so long. Life can be a challenge, but when we finally "open our eyes," we discover the beauty of it. Life is a true blessing, but we were so tunnel-visioned during our active addiction that we never took notice. Now we can see things for exactly what they are. Keep the faith that things will get easier. We do get to live a life of value that will make us joyous, happy and free.

One of the best moments happened last Christmas. After being estranged from my family for my dark years, I was actually asked to spend Christmas with them. I was nervous because we didn't really socialize because of my drug issues. I was so nervous that I almost canceled at the last minute, but my recovery requires me to get out of my comfort zone, so I went. Know what? I had the best time. It was so much fun watching my nephews and nieces unwrap their presents. I missed so much of their lives during my addiction that it hurt inside, but this special day made me feel like I was once again part of the family. Thank you, Alana, Patrick, Julie, Robbie, Colten, AJ, Ashley, Amber, Leland, and of course, the baby, Aliyah.

> "If you can't fly then run, if you can't run then walk, if you can't walk then crawl, but whatever you do you have to keep moving forward."—Martin Luther King Jr.

PRACTICING THE PRINCIPLES AND GIVING BACK TO OTHERS.

A Breakdown of the Twelve Steps of NA/AA.

Honesty—We admitted that we were powerless over our substance-abuse addictions and our lives had become train wrecks.

Hope—We finally believed that a power greater than ourselves could restore us to sanity.

Faith—We made a decision to turn our will and our lives over to the care of God as we understood him.

Courage—We made a searching and fearless moral inventory of ourselves.

Integrity—We admitted to God, ourselves, and another person the exact nature of our wrongs.

Willingness—We were entirely ready to have God remove all of these defects from our character.

Humility—We humbly asked God to remove our defects.

Reflection—We made a list of all persons we may have harmed, and we're willing to make amends to them if we can.

Justice—We made amends to whomever we were able.

Vigilance—We continuously took our personal inventories, and when we were wrong, we promptly admitted it.

Spirituality—We continued to pray and meditate to improve our spiritual development and our personal relationship with God as we understood him, praying only for knowledge of his will for us and the power to carry out his wishes.

Service—Having had a spiritual awakening as a result of working these steps, we brought this message to others and tried to practice these in all our affairs.

Helping others is a significant part of the AA/NA program, and there are many ways the program gets passed on to the next still-suffering addict. When you are living and practicing these steps and share it with others, you are actually carrying the message. Showing others that they can, and will, get better is always a blessing, especially after they learn how you battled back from the streets to take back your life. It will also help keep you sober. I believe it's our mission to help out others. Did we not receive help back when we needed it? I don't care how you get sober—AA/NA, Detox, SMART, MAT, Church—as long as you get sober and give yourself a chance at life.

Do not give up everything that matters in your life without a fight. Man up! Woman up! Your addiction is consuming you; it's taking over every piece of you on its way to destroying you. It will either kill you or imprison you in the end. This is your life we are talking about. Stand up against your addiction. You have the power to change your future right now. I can't make you change; that has to come from inside of you. You have to want to get better.

You can take the easy way out and ignore everything until you're a shadow of your former self, miserable, alone, broke. You can't blame society; you can't blame a crappy childhood or a crappy life. From this point forward, you own your decision on where you go from here.

Life is tough; it isn't fair. It never will be either. You will struggle, and you will have bad days. We used to use drugs to "escape" from our problems. Now, the reality of life is staring us in the face. I'm still struggling day to day, but I know for a fact that my life is so much better today because I am sober. I don't fear change. I don't fear failing either. Now I have the self-confidence to take chances that will improve my life down the road. On drugs, I couldn't do that; my addiction kept me from being me, and that is totally unacceptable now. Yes, society came knocking and wanted its due payback for my past life, and I owned what I did. I am making the changes needed today for a chance at a beautiful future. Our addictions were leading us down a path that many of us might not be able to bounce back from. It will always be there in the back of our minds, pushing for us to give it another chance to ruin our lives. Screw that BS.

Do not feed your addiction; feed your recover! You are never that far down the rabbit hole; you can get your life back—but only if you give up the drugs and stop feeding your addictions. Remember, Rome wasn't built in one day; you have the rest of your life to build something that you will be proud of. Repair those damaged and strained relationships. The future is out there, and we can't stop it from happening, but we damn sure can improve our chances at actually having a life worth living. Take it one day, one goal at a time. The following steps I am about to share with you will help you begin your own personal journey toward getting your life back. We all sort of know what causes our constant relapses, but I am about to list them in black and white for you. Some of these you may not be able to totally do, based on your current situation, but this is something we all have to figure out: how to adjust our current needs so we can have very best chance at recovery.

1. People, places and things. Yes we all have heard these terms over and over and over, but guess what? These are three of the main reasons we constantly fail at recovery. If we don't change these, then we're just

treading water in a sea full of sharks. We can make the excuses that we can't just walk away from our "friends and family," and maybe that's true. But we can limit our contact with the people who tear us down; we can limit our exposure to the places and things that give us nothing but bad mojo. You can support others who are still struggling from a distance. We must think about ourselves, about getting us better before we can help others find their way. Maybe you're stuck in a dead-end job and can't afford to move to a better location. My own journey of recovery has started in the same place that it started, the same place that I got high. It hasn't been easy to sober up there, but I am doing it. Each day, I face my demons in this house, and each day, I wake up early, go to work, and come home. Ten months recovery and going strong!

2. We need to build a foundation for our recovery. We must get outside our comfort zone and ask for help. Addiction will destroy us if we allow it another chance. Do not be afraid to enroll in rehab, detox, IOP, and/or get a sponsor. Change your thought patterns and learn how to change the ways you react to certain things. We can't continue to be the same if we hope to change our life. Try to catch your negative self-talk early and try to find the positive things that are happening to you. Eliminate things that are bad for you and start doing things that are good for you.

3. Work whatever works for you. Personally, I don't think there is a one program that fits all out there. I use NA/AA/SMART and mindfulness. Do whatever combination of recovery will keep you sober.

4. Work your recovery program and be willing to add new methods as they become available. We all had the desire to stop, but we just didn't know how to stop. Now we do and things will get easier each day. Stay focused on your recovery. Try to become a better person each day. Your addiction tried to change you inside, and chances are that it did change you. We must learn to take a deeper look inside of ourselves to find these destructive behaviors and correct how we react to them.

Got recovery? Recovery is the anytime "food for the soul." Thinking back to how I was and what it took to get my shit together, yeah, I'm grateful for being able to live my life the right way today. No more lying, cheating, or stealing; no more ducking the police; no more staying up for days, chasing something that was destroying me. Life is good today compared to what it was back then; that's something I will never forget. I will never let my addiction change me from who I really am. Life is too short for the BS, too valuable to waste doing things that don't feed your happiness. Got recovery?

One of my daily stops on my Facebook itinerary is a great group run by Ryan Hampton and Garret Hade called Voices to End Addiction and Inspire Recovery. This page has inspired thousands to share their personal recovery stories, which give me strength and hope. I highly recommend it for those of you on Facebook. It's a great page for everyone, and you just might be motivated to share your own personal story. I was.

A recent drug court graduation guest speaker, North Charleston Police Chief Reggie Burgess, gave a motivating speech about his own personal hardships growing up. He was adopted, raised by a younger mom that had to drop out of school and work two jobs to raise him and his two brothers. His rise to the top wasn't easy. He overcame much diversity to reach his current position. This is a great example of how all of us can bounce back from addiction and do big things in our lives. We are so quick to judge people who have these great lives and great jobs, without knowing the story behind how they got them. People will do the same toward each of us in our recovery, and they will judge us based on our past. Is it right? Should we accept the labels they put on us, or should we prove to them that people can change? I don't know about you, but my comeback from addiction is going to be such an amazing story. Your story can be right there next to mine. Together we can do this!

Self-rescue
Self-rescue can be described as learning to save ourselves when we are faced with a life-threatening situation. *Addiction is a life-threatening situation.* If we continue to follow blindly, then we are destined to die or be incarcerated. Period. There is no fairy-tale ending to that type of life. How do we self-rescue from these demons that live inside us? There is no softer, easier way for us to get better. Recovery is hard, life is freaking hard, and changing our thoughts and reactions is hard. Let me ask you this: was addiction easy? Sure—if you take away the costs, time, and everything else that you had to do to get the drugs. Most of us want to keep romanticizing how great the drugs made us feel. I can see that, but I refuse to forget all the BS that came with it. The guilt, the shame, the collateral damage it was causing to everything around me.

Sometimes we stay in active addiction because we don't want to feel the negative thoughts that accompany it, so we self-medicate. We "escape" to avoid dealing with life, and it just becomes easier to keep escaping than to face reality. It's a vicious cycle that never ends the way we intended, so what do we do? Self-medicate again. We slowly stop caring about anything. Addiction replaces who we were with a monster that only exists to feed our demons. That's the addiction matrix in its full glory—when we're willing to sacrifice anything and everything to do whatever it takes to keep the demons satisfied. Do you see the patterns yet? Once we can recognize the patterns, we can then prepare to defend ourselves against any future repeats. We take the strength away from our demons. We are learning to adapt to and overcome any potential future relapse. I call this being "enlightened." We can see how our past behavior affected our future behavior, and we can adjust accordingly. We avoid those unpleasant situations by being a step ahead of our addiction. If we notice any changes in our behavior, we go to a meeting or talk to someone who might understand what's happening. One of the most beautiful things about AA/NA is the motivation of "one addict helping another addict." Who better to help us navigate the troubled waters than someone who has been there?

If I told you that my belief is that all recovery roads lead us back to God, would you disagree? If I told you that you're angry with God about something you did with your own free will, would you still blame him? If I told you about his overwhelming, never-ending, reckless love for us, would you doubt me? Yes, I agree that the world can be a cold, unforgiving place. It's also a loving, beautiful place. His beauty is everywhere; our problem is that we allow ourselves to follow blindly what the media shows us; we buy the products that we know we shouldn't; we watch the TV shows that aren't healthy for us; and we allow our children to spend all their time "plugged" into violent games. We are becoming slaves to shiny things that catch our attention instead of becoming better people. I wasn't always this "guy." I chased it, drank it, smoked it, shot it, stole it, lied about it, and hustled innocent people, all in the name of the game. And I was selling my soul to the devil in the process. I was losing my true self to the "process" of addiction. Oh yes, addiction is a process too. It starts out recreational, but ask anybody in recovery how it spun out of control, sometimes quickly, sometimes slowly.

Eventually it consumes us all. Don't let that next high be the last thing in your life. Go home to your family; they miss the real you.

Three years ago, I didn't have a pot to pee in. I was angry, lost, confused, and battling a love/hate relationship with addiction. I can remember those days clearly because they were my fuel to keep moving forward. I wanted to change but did not know how to change. It's this confusion that keeps us hostage to addiction; it counts on us being scared and even intimidated by facing life sober. I was scared of what society would think of a guy who was broken and trying to make a comeback. I realized a few things rather quickly in my early recovery: you can't expect others to sympathize and forgive you automatically—because you're trying to get sober for the millionth time and you shouldn't be bothered by what others think. I quit letting society define me as an "addict," and I grew into something different. I am a person in recovery who's trying my best to stay clean and be a better person one day at a time. I don't care how you label me anymore because I'm here to be the best version of me possible. And if a guy like me can find happiness in recovery, then so can you. Yes! Take back the power! If a guy like me can do it, then anybody can. I went from "down and out" to living the life that I dreamed about. My life is not perfect, but it's better than it ever was. I'm not perfect in any sense of the word, but I'm better than I ever was. Recovery is a "work in progress" because we are all "works in progress." I'm sure you're scared of change. I was too, but each day, I showed up, and life got better. I got better. Believe that you can change and just do it. Walk the miles, ride the buses, attend the classes, and open the mind to what life can be—rather than what your life has been.

We talked about the "walk" toward recovery in regard to the physical/mental life changes, but today I want to talk about the "spiritual walk." Building a relationship with God—that's the ultimate game changer. Although our journeys are different, we are the same, and while we may agree that all recovery programs are different, I hope we can also agree that all roads lead us to God. Wear that armor of God and watch your demons lose their control over you and watch your life "level up."

We look at these amazing projects and marvel at their construction. Yes, their "construction," as they are being built from the ground up. And if you're like me, you curse at them for screwing up traffic, but as time goes by and the projects become finalized, we learn to appreciate the hard work that went into each one. Recovery is a project; you are constructing a new version of you. You are tearing down old ways and remodeling with new ways. It may not be pretty in the beginning, but that's ok; you're a work in progress. Keep building, and if you have to go back and start over to get it right, then that's what you do!

I get why some choose to recover in the secrecy of their home groups, and I respect that—just as I would expect you to support my right to not be quiet about my own journey. I believe the world needs to see that we can recover; otherwise, how would society change their opinions about people in recovery? How would people know who to reach out to if they needed advice on how to find treatment for their son or daughter? Addiction isn't going away. We were losing the battle before the pandemic, and you'd better believe nothing's changed. People are still dying at a ridiculous rate. I refuse to stay silent and pretend that everything is ok when I know it's a lie.

Silence isn't always golden. If we continue to be quiet about our recovery, then the message doesn't get heard by the ones who need to hear it. If we don't stand for something, then we stand for nothing. I stand for recovery. I know it's possible to overcome addiction because I am living proof. My addiction owned me, controlled me, and damn near destroyed me, but guess who is still standing? My recovery wasn't easy. I had legal problems (multiple felonies in multiple counties), I had family problems, and I had "me" problems. Hell, my problems had problems. I walked miles and rode hours of buses to make it to appointments, meetings, work. Every day my addiction told me that I would be back, it was telling me that I didn't deserve another chance. It laughed at me and assured me that nobody would ever love a loser like me. But guess who is still standing and fighting back? This guy. No matter what BS your addiction is feeding you, you deserve a life, you are loved, and you would be missed. You are only one decision away from a totally different life.

What you believe you can achieve. Everything. Who are you? Are you the hopeless son or daughter lost to the streets? Are you the mother or father who walked away from your children? Are you grieving a family member who died of an overdose? How do we bounce back? Why not keep running until we can't run anymore? We all fall down. What is your next move? Do nothing, and nothing improves. Do nothing and watch your life slip away. Do nothing and lose everything. It took me years to accept that I had a problem. Maybe I was finally being brutally honest with the counselors about hating my life and knowing that I couldn't go back out there because my life was becoming unlivable. I hated the entire process at this point; there was no more brief escape from anything anymore. I was tired—oh so tired of it all—and I just wanted to lie down and sleep until my life miraculously improved somehow. You don't know how damaged you are until you start thinking that death is a "good" option for escape. That's where my addiction took me, and I'm willing to bet that some of you experienced the exact same feelings at the end. But if you're reading this, you survived addictions endgame. My heart goes out to the families of the fallen ones who didn't break the addiction matrix

When, and only when, you decide you really want it, you will be successful. We can choose to ignore the truth, or we can embrace it then move forward. Addiction is a beast; it's powerful, cunning, and destructive. It will promise you the stars and deliver you to the gates of hell. And somehow, we still believe everything it tells us. It tells us we don't matter, that we are unlovable, and we begin to believe that's our destiny. Yes, I once did everything in my power to feed my addiction. I chose to ignore the truth about how it was destroying my life. I was ready to give up completely, and some nights, I prayed for death, all because my addiction wanted to claim another life. That's the addiction's master plan—to take everything from us before it delivers the grand finale. I'm not going to be a statistic. I'm not going to sit quietly on the recovery sidelines, hoping others will find their way back. I choose to carry my fight, to the gates of hell if needed. I want to stop the madness of addiction. I want to wake up those who are still lost in the addiction matrix. Today, I pray for life, mine and yours, and the strength to continue my fight.

Do you want to share your personal story of recovery? Your story can help another struggling addict! Email it to jrweaver0@gmail.com.

> The power of your story has the juice to change lives. A person gets their life back, a mom gets her son or daughter back, a child gets their mommy or daddy back.
>
> JR WEAVER

RECOVERY STORIES

Carrie

My name is Carrie Smith, and my story begins when I was twenty years old. I grew up in a structured, loving family. My parents are still together after fifty-three years of marriage, and we were provided with everything that we needed while I was growing up. I started weekend recreational using of cocaine, and it gradually consumed me until it was part of my everyday needs. I had some brief moments of sobriety while trying to take care of a family member up in Maine, and it was during this time that I had my son Logan when I was twenty-two years old. I thought this would have been the end of my "partying" days, but addiction doesn't work that way, and shortly afterward, I returned to active using.

    I started dating this guy and was introduced to OxyContin, and my addiction took off to another level. My life got to the point where I could not function without a substance in my system. I could not hold down a job to support my habit, and I had to start stealing from family members just to get my next fix. Legal problems soon followed, and my life took another bad turn when I was convicted of "accessory after the fact of armed robbery" when the guy I was living with decided to rob a *pregnant* cashier at the convenience store—because he had spent our rent money on drugs. I was found guilty and spent three years in prison, and yet this still was not my *rock bottom* moment. I finished my sentence, and I had promised myself that I would never go back to using drugs because of where it had led me. I thought switching from drugs to alcohol would be the answer to all my problems, and I was sorely mistaken. I am the type of person who could never take just one of anything, and it proved true during my drinking. I would drink until I blacked out and wake up not knowing where I was or what had happened the night before.

I would go several days without showering; personal hygiene was not a priority for me during my drinking days. I remember a few times when I drank so much that I woke up sitting in a puddle of my own urine. I also picked up two DUIs and do not even remember being pulled over. I remember going to work after a five-day binge and having to stay sober during my shift, and I started shaking really badly. My entire right side went numb, and I couldn't talk or write, so an ambulance took me to the ER. I remember the doctor asking me if I drank occasionally, and I said no because I was ashamed and did not want anybody to know that I had a drinking problem. I was not ready to give up the drinking, and part of me wanted to get prescribed some type of pain pills. I discovered that I had suffered a TIA (transient ischemic attack—or slight mini stroke) and a blood clot in my right arm, which caused me to be hospitalized for three days. I went right back to the drinking and eventually was fired from my job because of it. I still did not accept that I had a problem. A few weeks later, on July 21, 2016, my dad found me passed out face down in a puddle of my own puke, and he couldn't tell if I was alive or dead.

I remember my dad saying, "Carrie, you need to get your shit together. Get up and shower. Sober up. We're going to Mississippi to celebrate your grandmother's ninetieth birthday, and your son will be here in two weeks."

This was my rock-bottom moment, and I believe my dad saved my life that day because I have not touched a drink or a drug since then. I remember that the atmosphere of the twelve-hour car trip was filled with uncomfortable silence. I was detoxing by sweating, shaking, and vomiting, and I was miserable for the entire ride there. My life changed from that day. I got involved with a twelve-step program, found an incredible sponsor who would hold me accountable, and started working the steps. I struggled finding a job because of my criminal record, but I refused to give up hope.

I had worked in food and beverage my entire life, but I decided that I needed to change my career if I wanted long-term sobriety. I eventually was hired into a position that I had no experience with: a job requiring computers and office-job skills. It was very challenging, but I refused to give up, so I continued to show up each day with a positive attitude. The owner was ready to terminate me because I was failing at the position, but he was so impressed by my positive attitude that he changed my job. I spent two years working for him and being part of a wonderful work family. The business was eventually sold and closed, but I will forever remember Jeremy and the rest of my work family for all their support during my early recovery. Today, I work for my brother. I worked with him years ago and ended up stealing from his store to support my growing drug habit. Today, we have a great personal relationship, and we are involved in each other's lives. That is one of the true blessings of recovery.

When I started my recovery journey, for the longest time, I was quiet about who I was, in fear of social judgment, but today, I am not ashamed of who I am because the truth is that you never know who needs to hear your story. Today, I am incredibly open about my recovery. I want people to know that they are not alone and that we do recover. My passion today is helping others by letting them know that there is a better way of living free from the grip of addiction. I have just celebrated my fourth year of sobriety. Being in recovery has changed my life. I have a relationship with God and was baptized on March 30, 2019. I have a strong relationship with my family. I was able to be part of my parents fiftieth wedding anniversary, and I got to see my son graduate high school. I was able to get my driver's license back. I have also met this amazing guy, and we have this incredible relationship, going on two years.

George

Greetings from Greenwood, South Carolina, by way of the "Boogie-down" Bronx.

A little over a year ago, I was living homeless on the streets on NYC, searching for meals, men, a mattress, and my next fix. Sometimes, all four at one time. Addiction had become my full-time job. Meth had become my "rapacious creditor" and bled me of my self-sufficiency and all will to resist its demands. It seemed like there was absolutely no end to this vicious cycle, but I also didn't know (yet) any other way out. What I failed to see was that the number-one person standing in the way of this unknown, seemingly impossible, "joyous and free" way of life was me. In almost *every* way.

Today, after an introduction to a few simple rules, a few spiritual principles, and a reliance on a God for my understanding, I now work for the recovery center I went through. I have a car, a job, and a house to live in, but *most* importantly, I have my family, friends, my love of life, love for myself, and love for others.

By the grace of God, I have begun a journey back to sanity. I see colors more clearly than ever before, understand and practice (to the best of my ability) humility and compassion, recognize that there is always someone out there who has it worse than I do, and now have a message to carry—a message powerful enough to deliver someone out of inexplicable darkness, into a fellowship of light and life. And when I fall short, I acknowledge it, learn from it, correct it, and continue growing.

I am usually pretty humble about where I am in my recovery, but I am *proud of myself*! And for those of you committed to this new and beautiful way of life, *you should be proud of yourself too!*

We are worth it.

We can do it.

We can recover.

GOD CHANGES THE GAME TO A NEXT LEVEL LIFE.
JR Weaver

Asa

My name is Aislinne Langston, and I am a woman in long-term recovery. What that means for me is that I haven't had a drink or a mind-altering substance since June 21, 2018. I was born on June 15, 1980, in Moncks Corner, South Carolina. My parents were very young when I was born, with my mother being sixteen and my father being twenty years old. I didn't have a typical childhood experience. Both of my parents were addicts, and my mother was also alcohol dependent to boot. I was aware of the void that existed inside myself and tried to fill it by seeking attention from others—while trying to fit in with my peers at school. I was also tapped into my empath abilities at a young age, so other people's emotions and energies always had an effect on me.

    I never fully understood what it meant to be an empath and didn't know how to handle it. When I turned twelve years old, I was introduced to alcohol and marijuana and discovered that these substances allowed me to numb myself and my empathic abilities. From that point on, I started hanging around a lot of negative influences, which fueled my alcohol and drug addiction. I continued drinking and smoking weed until I entered the eleventh grade, when I was introduced to cocaine, as well as hallucinogens. I didn't attend school very often during my senior year and ended up getting pregnant at the age of seventeen. During my pregnancy, I was diagnosed with sciatica and was prescribed Lora-tab. Prescription opioids gave me an incredible high and, combined with cocaine, made me feel like I could conquer the world. During this time, I was surrounded by family members who both enabled and fueled my alcohol and drug addiction. I gave birth to a healthy baby girl I named Careleigh on November 3, 1998. By the grace of God, I graduated with the class of '98 from Berkeley High School.

I was able to get a job at local fitness center, working under my mother. My mother was also in active addiction, so I was able to fly under the radar and hide my addiction and alcoholism from everyone else. Fortunately, I was very successful and was soon promoted to the role of manager. During this period of time, I continued to use cocaine and hallucinogens while also getting involved with the underground rave community. I habitually took ecstasy and acid three to five days per week and continued doing so for years. Between 1998 and 2004, my addiction to opioid painkillers also escalated and led me to engage in doctor shopping around the Charleston area.

In 2004, I met a man named Michael, who was in the navy, and we ended up getting married in 2005. Marrying a man in the navy made it easier to obtain prescription opiates because we had good insurance and I was given greater access to prescribing doctors. Soon after we were married, we were relocated to Norfolk, Virginia, and my new husband went out on his first tour of Italy, which lasted six months. It was during this time that I was first introduced to heroin. Soon afterward, I ended up losing my heroin connection in Norfolk and was forced to drive to Charleston every two weeks to pick up drugs. It was at this point that my family started noticing a difference in my behavior and tried to intervene, but I wasn't willing to stop. I was delusional and didn't see that I had a real drug problem. My addicted brain told me I was ok because I had a husband, a child, a nice house, and a great car. At some point during those six months of my husband being on tour, I abandoned him and moved back to Charleston. Around 2006, I started using cocaine and heroin intravenously, and that's when my life really started spiraling out of control. I was like a trashcan-addict at that point and would use any substance in any form in order to avoid reality and run from the destruction I had caused by leaving my husband.

Coming back to Charleston, I found myself homeless, panhandling on the streets of Charleston, making hundreds of dollars a day. Eventually, I met another gentleman who was a cocaine/crack dealer and allowed him to support me and my drug habit. We were together for two years, and during this time, our lives totally revolved around the drug world. The relationship dissolved when he left me alone and without a supply of drugs. At this point, my survival instincts kicked in, and I started turning tricks to support my crack cocaine and heroin habit. I lived in abandoned houses, stayed at trap houses, and jumped from dealer to dealer to support my addiction. I was eventually introduced to Back Page, which enabled me to make loads of money because it gave me greater access to men in the market for sex workers. Soon, I ended up hiring other women and men to turn tricks, and I fueled their addiction by providing

them with and selling them drugs. I continued being a madam and selling drugs for five years while using heroin and smoking crack. I then met a group of local bikers, and they introduced me to the process of manufacturing methamphetamine. Not only was I addicted to drugs, but I was also addicted to making money, and I made sure I had plenty of it at all times.

In 2011, I lost custody of my eleven-year-old daughter due to my addiction, and she went and lived with her godmother. In November of 2017, after my daughter's seventeenth birthday, she found me on Facebook in hopes of reconnecting. I soon discovered that she had run away from her godmother's house, and she ended up living with me on the streets and in the motels of Charleston for six months. During that time, she was introduced to the lifestyle I was living and also the people I was affiliated with. On May 18, 2016, I got a phone call informing me that she had been in a car accident and that I needed to come to Trident Hospital immediately. I was in denial on the way to the hospital, and I told myself that the accident couldn't have been that bad. When I arrived, I was met by the chaplain, who informed me that my daughter was not going to live.

Sitting by her side that day in that hospital room, during the last hours of her life, was the most profound spiritual experience I have ever had. Feeling her energy leave her body made me realize that there was way more to this world and this life than drugs and the streets. Leaving that hospital, all

I wanted to do was get high to run from the pain, and I ended up living in active addiction for another two years. We buried her on May 21, 2016, and exactly two years later, I was arrested and locked up for the last time. I consider May 21, 2018 the day I buried my old self.

I really didn't get into too much legal trouble until I was first arrested at thirty years old. I would, however, go on to be arrested thirty-three times by the time I turned thirty-eight. I was charged with manufacturing, larceny, prostitution, driving under suspension, and distribution of heroin, among other things. In October of 2017, I caught twenty-two felonies for FTC fraud from using my sugar daddy's credit card. I was sentenced to drug court and put on probation in Clarendon County and transferred it to Dorchester County in Charleston, but I failed to report. When I got out this time, I said things were going to be different, and I was just going to use meth and abstain from using heroin. I got plugged in with a Mexican cartel for large weights of methamphetamine and worked with them for nine months until my last arrest on May 21, 2018. I said I wasn't going to use heroin, but eventually, I used heroin before my arrest. I took heroin and meth into jail with me and used until the drugs ran out after my first week. At that time, I was under the impression that I was going to prison for nine years because I had absconded from drug court and probation.

Once I'd detoxed from the meth and heroin I had brought in, my mind began to clear. I started seeking knowledge of the spiritual realm, reading a lot of self-help books, and practicing yoga and meditation in the recreation yard of Charleston County Jail. I was introduced to the twelve steps during my incarceration and started reading the *Big Book of Alcoholics Anonymous*. I was also baptized in Charleston County Jail on June 12, 2018, and I fully surrendered to my higher power. I had a couple of acquaintances come through jail with meth and heroin, and my last use was June 20, 2018. One night, I woke up in jail with a inexplicable burning sensation in my hands and feet that I had never experienced before. A couple of the older ladies on the rec yard told me it was a sign that my life was going to change and I would walk a different path. Little did I know that they were correct.

A couple of days later, my public defender came to see me and told me that the solicitor was offering me drug court again. I was released on October 8th, 2018, and I honestly didn't know any other life than the one I had been living before—selling drugs and living on the streets—so that's where I went. Two weeks after being released, I reached out to a dear friend of mine, and she recommended an Oxford House. I was at a crossroads where I could have continued my old way of life and run from drug court or taken a different path. Fortunately, I chose to take a different path. I was accepted into an Oxford House on October 18, 2018, and my life has completely changed since. I started going to meetings five days a week, I got a sponsor, and I started working the twelve steps. Since then, my life has done a complete one-eighty. The promises are a real thing! I have a relationship with my family again, I am a productive member of society, and I am enrolled in college, getting my associate's degree in art.

I plan on transferring to Charleston Southern to get a bachelor's degree in criminal justice, and I ultimately plan on getting my master's in psychology. I now have six sponsees that I sponsor through the twelve steps. The program has taught me to be selfless, and it has been a very humbling experience. I am no longer selfish or self-centered and strive to help the next sick and suffering alcoholic on a daily basis. I am an alumna of Oxford House now, and I am the Charleston Chapter chairperson and the state cochair. I help other sick and struggling addicts transition from the streets, institutions, and jails into sober living. I am graduating Charleston County Drug Court on September 9.

Today, I no longer have to numb myself from others' emotions and energies. I no longer have to fill the void with alcohol and other mind-altering substances. Today the void is filled with God. Reading all of those self-help books while I was locked away from the rest of the world helped me discover who I truly am. I realized what an empath is and was able to accept and love myself. Today I am able to feel other people's emotions and energies, recognize they aren't mine, and give it to God.

Leah

My name is Leah H., and I am a grateful recovering addict. My life forever changed on October 2, 2015, and I am eternally thankful. I got arrested for hopefully my last and final time. Throughout my life, I have made many mistakes. I have hit rock bottom multiple times and even found out it had a basement. Drugs and alcohol controlled my life for years, and I let them destroy me time and time again. I got started fairly young. I got drunk for the first time at ten years old. I was at a family event, and everyone was celebrating and getting drunk. So many adults offered me and my eight-year-old brother red cups filled with alcohol. We also kept sneaking them, trying to be cool like all the grownups we admired. By the end of the end of the night, everyone was drunk and acting the fool, including me and my little bro.

I've never seen anyone drink themselves "smarter." Most end up depressed, alone, and miserable. I should have learned my lesson then, but better late than never, I suppose. I continued drinking, though. If alcohol was left in the house, I would help myself to some and try to cover my tracks so no one noticed. Occasionally, my parents would let me sip their drinks on special occasions. By the time I was fifteen, I was an alcoholic—or "social drinker," as I called it. It's so heartbreaking how normalized alcohol has become. It's so common, it's everywhere; it's the legal drug that's been destroying families for years.

After alcohol, I started experimenting with benzos and pain pills. I even got suspended from school right before my sixteenth birthday for hanging out with my friends and taking pain pills for the first time. After that, my life continued to go downhill. I smoked marijuana for the first time at seventeen then graduated to experimenting with psychedelics and other drugs. I was eighteen years old when I moved away to another state and got in with the wrong crowd yet again. Eventually, I was introduced to heroin, and it was game over. Later, I found cocaine and meth, and the monster in me just grew stronger. I went from snorting dope to banging dope. I had watched people I grew up with, people I was extremely close to, get involved with drugs, and I'd sworn I'd never be like those people. And then I ended up being even worse than those people.

I knew better and did it anyway. I had seen it with my own eyes. I was raised in church and Christian school, and I still fell into the trap. Addiction does *not* discriminate, and it is out there, waiting silently to grab a hold of you. It comes to kill, steal, and destroy. It won't stop until it has done just that. It affects more people than we even realize. We are programmed from a young age that it's okay to have fun; you only live once. People want to rock and roll all day and party every night. Our music and idols teach us to drink, party, and live it up while we're here. They don't tell you the truth behind all of that, though: they don't tell you that you will never be satisfied, that you will always be wanting more. One is one too many; 1,000 is never enough. They don't tell you the nightmare behind addiction or where it really leads you. They don't tell you that it will overtake you—mind, body, heart, then soul—and completely own you. You will be a slave to this monster. It will always want to be fed. Your life will be about one thing only: your next hit or drink. You will live to use and use to live. You will hate your life, yourself, and everything. It will demolish you until there is nothing left. You will hurt everyone who loves you, mainly yourself.

They don't tell you about the withdrawals or that you'll lose everything. I never understood why I devoted my entire existence to living such a miserable, horrific nightmare. I've done things I never would have imagined just to get some dope—not even to get high but just so I could "feel normal." I never would have become that person sober. Drugs and alcohol promise you heaven and then take you to hell! It's a living nightmare, a vicious cycle. I was that lost cause, that addict who was never going to change. I should have died multiple times, but by God's grace and endless mercy, I am here to tell you that there is *hope*. We do recover. That day I got arrested, Oct 2, 2015, changed my entire life. I was possibly facing prison time, and I was so scared. This wasn't going to be just a slap on the wrist, like every other time, and it was exactly what I needed to open my eyes.

I was so angry when it first happened, but after I was in there for a few weeks, I realized I was my biggest problem. I had been holding myself back all those years by continuing to self-destruct rather than setting myself free. I kept myself in that hell, that prison, and only I had the keys to set myself free. I was sick and tired of the misery, the chaos, the endless, downward spiral. My way wasn't working. I realized that sometimes God wrecks your plans before your plans wreck you. Being in that jail cell gave me nothing but time to see that God had spared me and was giving me another chance at life, to do the next right thing. I felt so unworthy of everything life had to offer; maybe that was why I'd started using in the beginning—to numb myself from it all: the pain, the trauma, myself, life. I had done some awful things for my next high. I felt unforgivable.

Despite those feelings, I used my time to draw closer to God and try to really work on myself this time. Nothing changes if nothing changes, and I was tired of being a screw up. I read in the Bible about Paul. Before he found God, he was a murderer. He killed innocent people just for believing in God. I knew I had done some awful things in life, but I had never murdered anyone, especially not a Christian. That's insane! God used Paul despite all this. He saw Paul's drive for his cause and knew that, if he could change his heart, he could use him for the greater good. God can turn anyone's mess into a message. He specializes in that kind of miracle. Paul was used to write over half of the New Testament and bring many Christians to the light. I don't believe Paul would have had such motivation for the light if he hadn't experienced the darkness first.

God can bring your darkness to light as well. He did it for me. I was sentenced to probation and voluntarily agreed to seek help at a program. There, I met some amazing women. They helped me believe in myself and realize my true worth. Those women forever changed my life. As addicts, we need that connection; the opposite of addiction is connection. When I got out, I didn't stay involved with a support group and lost that connection. I slipped and started drinking again. My addict mind told me, "You know what to do differently this time; you've learned from your mistakes. Just drink beer and avoid liquor. Take your prescription pills for your mental health; they're nonnarcotic, and you need them. At least it's not heroin."

I quickly nipped that in the bud on October 28, 2016, and I haven't looked back since. Almost a year later, I created a Facebook group called Sober Sisters. It started with 200 members, and now it has reached over 8,700 members worldwide. A year ago, I was asked to help run another recovery page, #RecoveryRevolution. They had 100 thousand followers when I signed on, and now the number is over 238 thousand! God is not done! The lie is dead. We do recover! God took a beautiful disaster and turned it around for his glory yet again, and I pray he continues to do so. I pray He keeps using me and my soul tribe I found along the way to show the world that we *do* recover. God can use you if you let him!

I am grateful every single day that I made it out of the hell called addiction. So many others have died to this disease, and it breaks my heart every time I hear addiction claimed another life. Rest in peace to all those we lost, who left this world too soon. You are gone but never forgotten. This is a *huge* pandemic. I should have died to this disease multiple times, and I made it out only because I chose a new way to live. I chose to stop feeding my demons. I made a decision to leave that lifestyle and everything that came with it behind! It's been a long, hard road, but it is definitely worth it. You don't have to be another lost soul addiction has claimed. You don't have to die to this disease and become another statistic. Get out of the dope game while you still have a chance. Your life depends on it. Fight for your life! Chase your recovery like you chased the dope man! #SoberSisters #SoberSisterStrong #RecoveryRevolution #SoberFamily #SoberLife #SobrietySoDope #NoMudNoLotus #BeAHopeDealer #WeDoRecover

Sheila

My name is Sheila, and I am in long-term recovery. It's been a long, interesting, uncomfortable, painful, and at times lonely process. As I write this, my knowledge of addiction and mental health disorders still grows on a daily basis, as I do. My very first drug was diet pills in my mother's womb back in 1965. Tequila from a bar cart while my uncle was moving was the next substance—at the age of three. Neither of my parents consumed substances, but my dad was workaholic, and my mom was passive and naive. By the time I was five, trauma would appear in the form of my father shooting my dog with a shot gun and burying nine puppies alive. At nine, I came off a bus to find an uncle I didn't know packing our home and taking us from long island to New York City. Divorce.

I say now that fantasy was my first drug of choice because I could get lost and I didn't have to be me. I always felt like the new kid in the classroom. Unfortunately I usually was and by the time I was thirteen, my mom had remarried, and the stepfather trauma that included mental, physical, and sexual. Mom was in denial until today, 2020. Drugs came and went. I never liked to drink, never liked pot, never liked coke, etc. It wasn't until the early 90s, when heroin made it back on the scene in New York, that I fell in love. A cycle of hell, seventeen detoxes, one therapeutic community. It wasn't until I got arrested in 2005 in Brooklyn Supreme Mental Health Treatment Court that I stood a chance. I am one of the first 500 woman who was offered an alternative to incarceration. Unfortunately, relapse is part of this story—after five and a half years completing 350 classroom hours for the Casac, I made it back by God's grace and mercy. I completed the Recovery Coach Program. Today I am three years and seven months clean.

I'm all alone and feel I'm smothering.
It's because of the addiction I've been covering.
Why does the chaos never cease?
All I need is just a little peace!
I feel so beaten down and weak—Yet all day long it's drugs I seek.
Today I'll try a brand new scene. It's to my Heavenly Father I'll lean.
I prayed so hard with all my heart. I heard Him say, "You'll have a fresh start."
For now I'm held in His hand. Life is a lot easier to understand.
I'm not alone and no longer smothering. I'm just an addict truly recovering.

By Glenda Dean

Crissy

My name is Crissy Sinopole. My story is far from over; in fact, it has only just begun. For over twenty years, I wandered aimlessly, trying to accomplish my goals and live the dream we all desire to live, but a dark force within me would only let me go so far, and it pulled me back into outer darkness and despair. The darkness I never knew I battled against was addiction.

Throughout my life, unresolved trauma and generational dysfunction threatened to unravel my life. I could never see where I was going, and my self-sabotage came soon after. I put up big walls, which I'd built to protect myself, and viewed life through negative lenses; this safely became my defense mechanism. I had long periods of abstinence, went to treatments centers, and did programs. All of it helped me stay sober—but with no real joy or longevity. Every struggle or bump in the road became an excuse to use and a chance to blame—until I hit my last rock bottom. I was facing mental, spiritual, and possible physical death. That day, I could barely whisper as I tried to bargain with God to help me. I promised him that, if he would me, I would help others just like me. God heard my prayer that day.

Today, I no longer live in abstinence. I live in full active recovery mode twenty-four, seven, with no time off. I protect my recovery and guard my heart and peace of mind. Because I am working an honest program built on functioning morals, values, and spiritual principles, freely giving out and making room for more—my life is miraculously changing.

Today I see that, even though my heart always had the right intentions, nothing ever worked because I was a broken soul that needed inner healing. If life was good, I'd quickly have to cause a disruption because good was unfamiliar and bad was safe. The true warriors are the people God has placed in my life who've unselfishly spent time to support and encourage me. I've been able to see my value and worth. We hear it often, but it is so true: if God can change someone like me, a poster child for failures and fall-downs, a societal reject, anything is possible.

The one person I had to learn to love was myself. Since doing that, I've claimed the innocence I lost as a child, and I continuously endeavor to turn every struggle, fall, and failure into a lesson for growth. I live a transparent life with no shame because there is life after addiction. I am not anonymous!

Wendy

My name is Wendy, and I am a recovering addict. I am a firm believer in what substance-abuse counselors call "dual diagnosis." Dual diagnosis is the treatment of underlying mental disorders coupled with substance-abuse disorder. I believe that my spiraling addiction began with life events I couldn't cope with. In high school, I was a highly regarded scholar attending the FBI Youth Leadership Program, a highly decorated JROTC officer and commander, a willing participant in ride-alongs with the local police department, and a police cadet with an internship at the local sheriff's office—all in preparation to become a future FBI agent.

My senior year in high school, I found out I was adopted. This event turned my life around, and I did not know how to cope with my feelings. I was eighteen years old. Was my whole life a lie? Who was I, and where had I come from? I withdrew from school (with enough credits to still graduate) and began running with the wrong crowd, having fun, and partying. I smoked weed for the first time. I began drinking socially. Then I graduated high school. The summer after graduation, I experimented with cocaine, x, acid, and more marijuana. I ended up getting my act together later in the year and joining the military. I could've received scholarships and gone to college, but after withdrawing halfway through my senior year, I neglected to fill out any college applications, apply for any scholarships/financial aid, or work with guidance counselors to further my education.

All I wanted to do was to be free and party. Mistake number one—as I am now thirty-seven years old with only a high school diploma. The military didn't do much to keep my partying at bay. I somehow always attracted the wild crowd and did all the same drugs mentioned above, just in moderation so I could pass a urinalysis.

Two years in, I married a local boy I knew from back home who ran with the same wild crowd I'd left to get away from. I moved him to California with him, continuing my military career, only for him to develop depression nine months in because he "missed his friends and his life back home." I went AWOL, thinking it would allow me to get out of the military and move home. I was afraid he would leave me, and I was still a newlywed and very much in love, not wanting to separate. After receiving military punishment, I was discharged from the army, and we began the cross-country trip to move back home to South Carolina and be happy together. Mistake number two.

Shortly after moving back to South Carolina, I became pregnant with our first daughter. Life was a struggle, but we were making it one day at a time, still smoking weed, drinking, and consuming the occasional bag of cocaine to keep ourselves happy. Two years later, our second daughter was born. At this point, I no longer used x or acid, and I barely drank alcohol. Life was still a struggle, and then I landed a job as a bank teller. Daycare, bills, partying, and raising two young daughters was stressful, but we still managed with the help of family. Of course, my family didn't know the extent of my drug abuse, and I lied to them and hid it for years, all the while accepting their money to pay my bills because my bill money went to the drug man.

My children grew up and began public school. I continued my career in banking, getting promotions and making more money. My husband's salary grew, as did his alcohol consumption and our mutual drug consumption. I was proud of my job, moving up the ladder, but somehow I still wasn't completely happy, and I didn't understand why. Looking back now, I realize it was because I was hiding a drug habit, getting money from my parents by lying about where I spent my money. I wasn't proud of myself. Over the course of our marriage, we had many fights and arguments. In 2007, my husband punched me in the face after a night of drinking and went to jail. This was his first CDV charge, and it was followed by 6 months of anger management and promises to tame his daily drinking habit. Lies.

In 2009, eight years into the marriage, prescription drugs entered our lives. This was the beginning of my end. It began with me being bored on the weekends when my husband and I would invite friends over. They would drink and get drunk, and I would be sober. His alcoholism turned me off to drinking, so that was a good thing. I would get bored watching everyone, until I was offered a Lortab. I took it, and thus began my weekend habit. Unfortunately, my sister-in-law, who was twenty-four at the time, liked them a little too much. She overdosed and passed away in early 2010, leaving behind my brother-in-law and their two young kids. Tragic.

Her death slowed my consumption for a little while and made everyone more cautious, but it didn't stop me. My husband and everyone around me all fell prey to the euphoric high of prescription drugs. This habit continued until our downfall in 2015. By 2015, I had been in banking almost ten years and married for fourteen years, and my children were twelve and ten years old. My husband and I had a daily pill habit and weed habit, along with his daily alcohol habit. During this peak, our drug habit cost us an average of one hundred dollars a day. Our marriage began to suffer, with arguments and verbal abuse becoming an everyday occurrence. We fought, argued, broke things, called each other names, got in each other's faces, and even became physically violent, all in front of the children. My life was miserable. I began an adulterous affair with a neighbor, and my husband found out and punched me in the face, giving me a black eye. I began using a lot of sick time and even had to explain my abusive home life to my boss after reporting to work with a black eye. My in-laws had enough and called DSS and turned us in for criminal domestic violence and drug abuse in front of the children.

My girls were sent to live with my in-laws, whom I now despised because they'd turned me in. I ended up quitting marijuana in September 2015 but couldn't shake my pill addiction. It consumed me. I blamed everyone else for my troubles, not the drugs. During a visitation with my children, I spit in my father-in-law's face, and he called the cops and got a warrant for my arrest. A week later, I was arrested at my job for third-degree assault and battery, which subsequently led to my termination. I had lost my children, my marriage, my job, my self-respect, and the respect of my peers and family.

I moved out of my home and moved in with my lover. I fought and won unemployment but still struggled. I fought CPS and fiercely defended my character, all while still taking six to eight pills a day. A few months went by, and I noticed red flags with my lover. He seemed depressed and spoke of suicide a few times, but I didn't understand mental disorders at the time. I mean, I couldn't even figure out what was wrong with my own self! On Christmas Eve 2015, I argued with my lover and stepped outside to smoke a cigarette for about fifteen minutes. When I was done, I returned to the bedroom and found him hanging in the closet. He didn't make it. I was in shock and traumatized. I moved back to town and met up with old friends, who introduced my most recent demon: methamphetamine.

It was cheaper than pills, and it eventually weaned me off my pill habit. So I switched one habit for another. Now I was a meth user. I was unpredictable and impulsive on meth. I concocted a plan to kidnap my children, which was a brief success—or so I thought. My children were put in the foster care system and separated. I was sad that I'd lost everything and took drugs to cope, only realizing later that the drugs were hindering me. My mother became sick, and that was another burden I had to bear, which also prevented me from getting clean because I was self-medicating a depression I didn't realize I had.

The drugs had clouded my mind and my choices. My mom passed away in February 2017. This was the catalyst of my healing and sobriety. I began taking drug classes at the VA in March and got clean. Working with the housing program at the VA, I eventually got my own apartment in July 2017 and was awarded custody of my children in August 2017. After getting sober, things began to work out for the better. As I look back now, I can see that I was depressed for a long time and never realized it. Now I am happy, sober and rebuilding my life. My only regrets are the two years I missed with my children and that my beloved mother passed before I was able to make her proud. Life lessons sometimes run deep. These are mine, and I can finally tell my story, as that chapter in my life is finished. Thanks for reading.

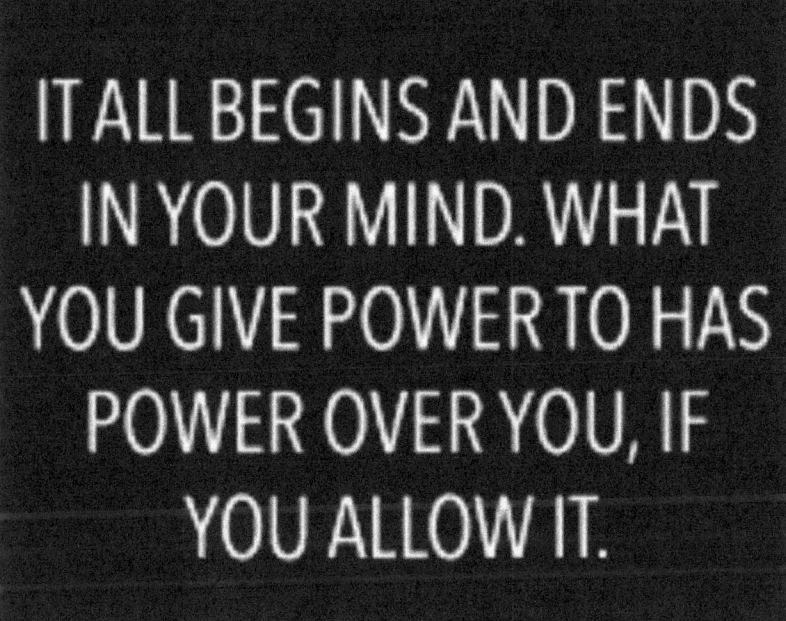

Angela Delmar

Hi, I will tell you my story if you'd like. And I don't mind if you share it. My name is Angela Delmar. I was born in Riverside, California. My father was in and out of jail until I was nine. My mother was never around. Every once in a while, she would come take one or two of my siblings, so she could collect welfare, then drop us back off with my grandma. I watched my dad get stabbed in front of me when I was five. I watched the cops come arrest my dad and my uncles. When I was nine, my dad went to treatment in Washington, and so my grandma, my siblings, my dad's girlfriend, and my youngest brother's mom moved in with us. Life was semi-ok. Then when I was fourteen, my brother committed suicide in juvenile detention. Not long after that, we found out that my second-to-youngest brother and oldest brother weren't my dad's and that my biological father wanted them back.

    I was physically and mentally abused by my grandma, so I was a bit out of control. I would run away and do drugs and alcohol. My dad sent me to California too. At this time, I was still fourteen. My biological mom was never around, my oldest brother had joined a gang, and I was stuck taking care of my youngest brother, who was nine. My biological mom sold me to grown men so she could get her next fix. I was molested, raped, and abused. I had to rob men to get money to eat and feed my brother. I was deep into drugs. Luckily that only lasted for seven months. Then I ended up back in Washington with my dad.

    I checked into my first treatment center at the age of fifteen. I grew up a lot after treatment but only stayed clean off drugs for a while; I still drank a lot. I got pregnant at seventeen and had my daughter at eighteen. I also started doing meth heavily at eighteen. A good friend of mine died in front of me by dropping a sawed-off shotgun in my apartment. My daughter's father became abusive, and I ended up having my son at twenty and stayed with my kid's father for almost five years. He left me for another chick. I didn't know what to do without anyone telling me what to do, so I ended up in treatment for six months. I stayed clean for about a year. We ended up having CPS involvement, and I ended up pregnant by this loser plus I was strung out. So the options were sign over my two kids to their father or lose them. I signed them over. Then he ended up hiding my kids from me for about three years. I ended up having my third child. My third child's dad made me have sex with him before my stitches were even out, and I got pregnant right away. I have five kids. I stayed with my younger kid's father for seven years, being abused physically and date-raped emotionally and mentally. I sold drugs to survive. I ended up with all of my kids. My youngest kid's dad molested my kids, so I left my kid's dad and reported it. I ended up leaving my oldest two kids with my brother and his wife because I really had nowhere to go. I got into another abusive relationship. My brother ended up abusing my daughter, so I ended up taking my older two kids back and reported my brother. My five kids and I lived with my abusive boyfriend in a travel trailer with no privacy. We stayed there up until my boyfriend at the time choked me to the point of passing out in front of my kids. I ended up losing my kids. I was strung out and intoxicated all the time. I was hopeless and tired of living. I wanted to die but didn't want to kill myself. So I would hitchhike from Washington to Nevada and back. My walk was so drunk down dark highways. I gave up hope of getting my kids back.

I had an amazing friend, Pam from Alaska. I remembered her asking me if I wanted to move to Alaska and go to treatment. At the time, I hadn't wanted to but now I did. So I got a hold of her, and she said she would help me. I don't think she thought I was serious, so I told her I would end up in Alaska at the airport; this way, she would have no choice but to help me. And I did. July 17, 2017 is my clean date. Two weeks later, I went to a twenty-eight-day treatment facility at Serenity House in Soldotna, Alaska, on the highest tier level. I went from treatment to Freedom House ran by Jennifer Waller, a Christian-based home for women like me, trying to find their way in life.

I stayed there for a couple months then lived with my friend Pam. I found Jesus, found out who he is and what he's done for us, so I decided to become a follower of Jesus Christ. I was baptized on January 14, 2017. I moved back to Washington on January 26. I am still clean and am getting my kids back. All five of them. See, recovery is possible, but you have to work hard to stay clean. I got a sponsor. I do step work. I go to meetings and involve myself. In fact, I'm attending a NA meeting in Cathlamet, Washington.

ADDICTION RECOVERY and YOGA

How people have used yoga as part of their journey in recovery programs from serious addiction problems to a new life of well-being and emotional stability.

TODAY IS THE MOST IMPORTANT DAY IN YOUR RECOVERY.

JR Weaver

Olivia

One year clean and sober today! I can't even believe it! What an amazing journey it's been so far! And that's the beautiful part of this. This journey is not over; there are so many more amazing blessing, and God's grace is in my path! I've been a chronic relapser a long time, but when I truly surrendered my life to God and let him take over, he proved that his way is so much better than mine!

This has been one of the most amazing days of my life, and if I keep relying on God I'll have many more! I used to see others pick up year chips, and it just seemed like a fantasy that would never come true for me. But I put my life in God's hands, and that fantasy became a reality one day at a time! Thank you, everyone, for the love and support! I also want to give thanks to my little dog, Heaven Nevaeh. She is also a big supporter of my recovery!

Opportunity of Today

"You have precisely one opportunity to live this day well. That opportunity is now, so act on it now.

"If you want this day to bring value, then give it value. Now is when you start.

"Right now you can establish positive momentum. And you can continue to feed that momentum with action.

"Think of the most productive, successful day you've ever lived. As you recall and feel the reality of that day, commit to make today even more productive, even more successful.

"Within you right now is the ability to make this the best day yet. Within you right now is the willingness to push your life to a higher level than ever before.

"Act now with that ability, with that willingness, with your knowledge, skills, and resources. Now, embrace and enjoy the unique opportunity of today."—Ralph Marston

> i'm not telling you it is going to be easy, i'm telling you it's going to be worth it.

Briana

By far heard the best words from a friend I help get into a treatment. Hearing the words "You were a part of saving my life" is by far the most amazing feeling. God truly puts people into your life for a reason. There is no better feeling than being a part of someone's recovery.

Cricket

Yesterday, I stood in the rain at a ribbon-cutting ceremony after having been asked to share my story. I was given some bullet points of the things they would like me to say. (Side note: I've never been good at adhering to bullet points when speaking.)

So, as I stood there gathering my thoughts in the rain, I was taken back to March 22, 2017. On that date, I was standing on a corner in Richmond, Virginia, in the rain, dope-sick, and holding a sign that said, "Smile. It could be worse; this could be you…"

I had reached "rock bottom." Panhandling and doing whatever illegal or immoral acts it took to get the next drug/drink—this is what I had found myself willing to do. My disease had taken me hostage, and I had one responsibility: get more.

My girlfriend and I, both from good homes with good families, were staying at my mom's house briefly. We had recently been kicked out of the sober-living houses we lived in because we chose to get high "just one more time." This turned into almost nine months of insanity. My mom, being the saint that she is, told me that she refused to watch me kill myself and that I needed to get clean or get out, bless her heart.

So, I left her home to live in my car…in the winter…in Virginia…with only enough gas to run the heater or make it to the dope man in the morning. My tires were bald, my license was suspended, I was broke and unemployed, and man, was it cold! We lay in that freezing car for a few weeks, sacrificing our needs to get our wants. My disease had me convinced that I was "being responsible" by making sure we could get high in the morning, instead of staying warm at night.

In the midst of the opioid epidemic, people were overdosing daily, some in my presence, and still I couldn't stop. After several fruitless attempts to "just quit," I realized I was in trouble and needed to do something different. So on March 22, 2017, I made a decision to change and call for help.

One year ago today, I flew across the country to San Diego to enter a thirty-day treatment program. There, I was able to surround myself with people like me and a staff that truly cared about my recovery. My intentions were to eat up the five days' supply of detox meds that were provided and spend the next three weeks trying to figure out a plane ticket to get back home.

God had a different plan, and I'm so thankful that he did! When I discharged, I moved into a sober-living organization. I began attending twelve-step meetings regularly and practicing a daily program of recovery. I surrounded myself with the "good herd" and remained open to their suggestions for growth. This has provided me the foundation I need to regain the strength and courage it takes to be truly responsible for the outcome of my decisions—which have thus far provided a life that I didn't think I deserved.

Recovery continually offers me things that I never thought were possible.

Relationships are mending—not only do people answer my calls now, but they actually call me sometimes too!

Confidence is returning. I am able to look at the guy in the mirror and actually like him. I can go to bed at night, *knowing* that today I tried to be my best self. I am financially self-sufficient; I am able to enjoy when I've just paid a bill on time, taken a newcomer out to lunch, booked a flight to visit family, or filled my gas tank up.

Recovery allows me to be employable, trustworthy, trusting, honest, reliable, and willing. Most importantly, I am able to be a face and voice of recovery and provide hope and direction to those who are desperately trying to live a better way.

If you are out there, in active addiction, slaving away to get "more," I *have* to let you know that there is a better way. There is a good life that may be unimaginable to you right now, up for grabs, in recovery. Give yourself a break. We'd love to have you on the team!

Today, a year after my last "high," I am truly grateful for my recovery process and the people in it. I *knew* that I couldn't do it alone, and you guys convinced me I didn't have to...

Tim

What an amazing sense of a power greater than myself. By being honest and sharing recovery experiences that other people relate to and share also. I am open about my recovery from addiction and colorectal cancer. Had it not been for an awakening that I had very little to do with, I would have died back in 1982 by suicide. That was the beginning of my addiction recovery. Had I died, I would have never been diagnosed with cancer in 2013. Both are serious and fatal without help. Oddly, I see myself as blessed. Not because I am still around. It is because this power has taken something so potentially devastating and given me an avenue to provide support and experience to others. I now get why Dr. Bob, in an effort to continue his sobriety, impacted over five thousand other alcoholics. He simply channeled his fight into love and service. The magic, he humbly said, came from a loving, forgiving God. So I guess it is not what we do in a material sense. It is about establishing and expanding an open channel for this loving, forgiving God. The door to this experience for me is contained in the principles, steps, traditions, and absolutes of a twelve-step design for living. The resulting friendships and love have shown me a very valuable insight about my life. It is not about me and what I face. It is about being an honest and open person who is willing to let the power flow and guide others toward a life with purpose and meaning that we never thought had any worth. Our heartfelt experiences. They lead us to another sense of amazement. Unity through simple acts of service and love. This is the God we share.

JR Weaver

I'm a guy in "lifetime" recovery who found, through the grace of God, a better way to live. I grew up in a "normal" family, but there was always something that felt empty inside. My story, like most of yours, started out when I used drugs as a recreational thing, and before I knew it, the drugs were using me. It started with the alcohol and having to drink to feel normal, then when the alcohol stopped working, I switched to drugs. Weekend binges turned into weeklong binges, and I became a prisoner to my addiction. My life started deteriorating immediately, so I increased my drug usage to make myself numb. I started using every day, even during working hours. Somehow I still thought I was in control of my usage. That's what my growing addiction was telling me, so I believed it and blamed everything else that was going wrong on just bad luck. I remember my roommate at the time had left a new credit card lying on the table. Normally, I wouldn't have paid any attention to it, but money was running low, and I needed my daily fix, so I "borrowed" it—that's what my addiction was telling me.

Well, he found out, and I was asked to move out. I was still in denial and didn't blame the drugs. At my job, my boss started to notice my lack of productivity, not to mention all the sick days I was borrowing. I was terminated. Denial became my best friend. Still, I couldn't blame my addiction. Just another bad break, right? I had started to write bad checks to get cash. My bank account balance, after all the bounced checks every week, was averaging about a negative thousand dollars. My payday direct deposit would temporarily clear my account, and the cycle would begin again. I needed my drugs; nothing else mattered.

I started to think I might have a problem, so I changed locations. I moved back to South Carolina to be around my family. People, places, and things, right? I thought I had left my addiction and bad memories up in Connecticut. After a few sober days, my addiction was back. What would a little bump hurt? I had already proved to myself that I could go a few days without it, so I believed I could quit it anytime. No job, no money. I went back to what I knew worked, writing checks! After a few months, my luck finally ran out, and I faced massive fraudulent check charges. I was sentenced to eight months in prison.

Guess who was waiting for me when I finally got out? My addiction was there with open arms; it didn't judge me, and it helped me forget about the past. Looking back now, I can finally own that my decisions were leading me down a road that I'm blessed to be sharing about. It's crazy to think we take drugs to lose ourselves because we may not be happy, but ironically, it is the drugs that make our lives even crappier. I started running the streets, trying to hustle to get my drugs, but it was never enough. I tried to clean up a few times on my own, but eventually, I always fell victim to my demons. I would often find myself questioning my life. What was I doing with it? I was so far down the rabbit hole that I couldn't see a way out. That's where addiction wants to keep you.

My dad passed away in 2015, and I turned down the opportunity to spend time with him before he passed because my addiction was my first priority. My addiction couldn't risk losing me, so I never got to see my dad before he passed. That guilt has been eating me ever since. (I'm sorry, Dad. I almost screwed up my life chasing things that were destroying me inside and out. I hope you can see me today, sober and leading a positive life.)

After catching some new serious charges, I finally had to ask for help. I joined a homeless and rehab program. I did the meetings and classes with renewed determination; I just knew that I could turn my life around. I was semi-committed, so how could I fail? I graduated the programs, got myself a crappy little apartment on the edge of the hood—and guess what my addiction told me on my first night alone? "You can do just one. Nobody will know. You can control it." Well that "one" turned into four months of using and four extra felony charges before I was done. I had pleaded into drug court for felony charges in two other counties; now I had four more felonies in another county. I had to make a choice: addiction or a life free of drugs. For years, I'd let my guilt and shame keep me in active using. It took me a long time to accept that my past was over and living in regret for the things in my past wasn't going to help me heal. If I wanted to get better. I needed to forgive myself. I needed to be able to love myself again if I ever expected to make the greatest comeback in my life. Yes, it was tough letting go of my anger and fears, but in the end, I know my little girl would want me to quit using her as my excuse.

Back in my early stages of addiction, my girlfriend got pregnant, and do you think we stopped using? That wasn't enough to get us to stop! We kept using with the excuse that we would stop tomorrow, but tomorrow never came, and we kept using like addicts in denial do. You can probably see where this is going: we lost our daughter because we couldn't stop using. Emily Crisanta Weaver. My biggest and darkest secret. Guess what my response was? To self-medicate and make myself numb to the pain that I felt inside. How was that not enough to make me want to quit? That's how powerful addiction is!

I have held on to this guilt since September 11, 2003, and I believe I have let myself suffer enough. I am now willing to do whatever it takes to turn my life around this time. (Emmy, I hope you're proud of me today). I was blessed to have drug court on my side, and they helped roll my new charges into my plead. Today I am sober because I made a choice to live a clean life. I am repairing my strained personal relationships that suffered from my addiction, and I am working again. Life is good, and I am happy today.

I still do the drug classes and meetings. If you're reading this, then I hope you will realize that addiction will control your life and destroy you. It doesn't care what you have to do to get high. If you get incarcerated, it will wait patiently for you to get out. Do not waste twenty years of your life, like I did, before you wake up to the reality that addiction isn't your friend. I now accept that, if I want a life, then I can never do drugs ever again. And you know what? I am completely happy with that. I have my family back. I have "me" back. Life is so much better when you're not shackled to substance-abuse issues. Give yourself a chance at a real life and get some help. Open yourself up. Don't let your demons own you anymore. Hell, if a once-hopeless addict like me can do it, then you should be able to do it! Why put myself out there like that? Because I want to help others see the light and get back their life! Thank you for reading this and good luck!

I am thankful for this opportunity to have a life and grateful for my fiftieth second chance to get my shit together. This past year has been...amazing. I feel like my eyes, mind, and heart have been opened. I've seen the light, and my past is just that: in my past. I sat around all weekend trying to write the final chapter of my book, but now I realize that the only perfect ending is to keep doing what I've done every day: wake up sober with a clear conscious. To keep leaving the light on for others who seek recovery from their own demons. If I can break those last few threads of resistance for them, then it's all worth it. Nobody should have to live like that. Get your ass home to the people that love you. The drugs and alcohol don't.

On November 11, 2018, I celebrated my first year of sobriety at the Blue House in Charleston, South Carolina. I love my new life, free from active addiction, surrounded by positive people that care for me. One year, 365 days—once upon a time, I didn't know if I could make it twenty-four hours, but here I testify that it's possible, even for someone who once considered himself hopeless and doomed to spend the majority of his future behind bars or eventually dying in a hotel room. There is no future in drug addiction outside of jails, institutions, or death. Drugs and alcohol don't love you. Your family and true friends do. It's time to grow up, time to go home and take back your life. I couldn't have reached one year of sobriety without all the positive support from everybody. Thank you all so much! Let's go get another year!

Sober and happy today! Sober strong!

> You're going into a season where you're about to experience breakthrough after breakthrough because what you went through didn't break you.

Amanda

My name is Amanda Timberlake, and I'm thirty-five years old. It all started when I was thirty-one. I started hanging out with this guy that I knew was trouble, and he was doing things I said I would never do. But I told myself that, if I started hanging out with him, he would change his ways and be different and stop doing those things! I was so wrong! A friend and I were hanging out with this guy one night, and he pulled out a bag of meth. I got nervous at this point because the only drug I had ever done or tried was weed! I had never been in trouble or had any kind of record before, so being around meth was all new to me. I had heard only bad things about it, so needless to say, I was scared, but at the same time, I wanted the guy to like me. That's when I tried it.

I didn't feel anything right away, but I know I was up for seven days and working a full-time job. I was able to still work my job and function at the start of my drug use! I was able to still parent my three kids, who were old enough to know what was going on. I ended up in a relationship with this guy who was cooking the drug called meth, and we would do the drug he was cooking! It became an everyday thing, and as the days went by, things started getting a little more difficult. I found myself running late to work, acting as an unstable parent for my kids, as I just thought they were ok with my mom and stepdad. The guy and I started fighting, and he became abusive, and I would make excuses about why he would put his hands on me—it must've been something I'd done.

We spent our days selling and cooking drugs, as I had learned every step to making meth. It seemed that every day got worse, and I found myself getting further away from my kids and family, the ones that loved me most! I would make excuses for letting days go by without seeing my kids (who were my everything). And when I did have my kids, they didn't want to be around me because my partner and I would fight and scare them! I was becoming someone I didn't know; I was doing things and acting in ways I never would have imagined. I would steal things out of stores because he would or because we had no money—it had all gone into buying the items needed to make the drugs. It got so physical with me and this guy that he gave me a black eye, and I stayed with him, not calling the cops and making excuses that it was ok and he still loved me. He knocked out three of my front teeth in front of all three of my kids by throwing an air freshener can at me from a distance. I had to get stitches and walk around without three of my front teeth for two years! But I still thought he loved me, and I stayed with him!

There was not a day that went by that was a good day! I went to jail and got felony drug charges because I was involved with this guy, and I don't put all the blame on him because I made my own decision. But if it was love, he would not have been wanting me around the things he had going on! I was the driver in my car when we got pulled over. In the car there were drugs, fuel for meth, pills used to make meth, weed, and other items. I think we were on day three of no sleep, and there were five of us in the car, and no one would own up to the items, so we all went to jail for a few days.

In jail, I said that I was done with him because he could not even take the blame for his own things. My car was impounded, and my parents had to pay to get it out. (Mind you, my parents were not happy and did not support this lifestyle.) We all got out of jail at the same time, and I still left jail and went home with him, even though I had a way out—because my mom was there waiting on me. I still chose the wrong direction by my own choice. The guy ended up having previous charges catch up with him, and he got prison time. At this point, he got arrested in the court room, and I thought it was the worst thing at that point, not knowing it was the best! I think it was a few hours before I got a three-minute call from him, and during that call, he was telling me how much he loved me and needed me during this time.

I was sure I was going to be there for him and support him, and I did not even have a job. I was staying in his trailer, which had no heat, and his power ran from a drop cord connected to his parents' house next door. Needless to say, the place should have been condemned! It was definitely a meth cook's house! The meth fumes were so bad, there were rusted the metal objects in the house due to the very bad chemical smell! I continued to stay there while he was locked up, but at this point, I found myself cooking meth several times a week to make the money to support him in jail. I would ride around selling the drugs to his people and basically putting myself in places I did not need to be. Then I would still hear him fuss when he called because $200 on his books every other day was just not enough!

I was running myself dumb for him, and again, it was not all his fault because, at this point, he had no control over me; he was locked up! I was hooked on the easy money and addictive product. Everyone was wanting it from me. I felt like I was actually wanted or needed, but looking back now, I was selling people the devil! After about four months cooking meth and selling, I ran into a guy that I had worked with before and started selling to him. He and I became really close, and we were both in relationships, but neither of us was happy or where we wanted to be.

I continued to sell to him on a daily basis, and we became closer. There, I found a way to end my relationship with the guy in prison. I started gaining feelings for this guy named Mikey, and he made me feel loved and cared for. It opened my eyes to the relationship I was leaving. I told the guy in prison that I could no longer be with him and that I was talking with another guy, and of course, that was fire to his ears, and he just did not want to hear that!

Mikey and I both ended the relationships we were in, and we became closer! Drugs were still a part of our relationship, but it was different because Mikey helped me get my relationship back with my kids. He wanted to do things with my kids and me—not just me or the drug. The kids started staying on the weekends with us. Mikey and I had moved in together, and I was still cooking, but it was different; neither of us really wanted to cook, so that slowly stopped, but we continued to sell and do drugs! My boys were with us all the time at this point and saw more than they should have. On school nights, if we had to make a drug run, they would sleep in the back seat of the car while we made a deal. Most mornings, I would wake up at the last minute to get them ready for school and rush out the door, just to come back home and sleep until they got out of school!

Our life pretty much started at night, and that's when we ran the roads! My boys could tell you what drugs were and what they looked like! It was getting bad for Mikey and me, with sleepless nights and steady night runs. We would fight in front of the kids, say things no one should ever say, not even to their worst enemy! The boys would step in between us, yelling to try and stop us from fussing. We would make up and then, a day or so later, be back fussing again! It was just a never-ending cycle! One fight was so bad that we knew we couldn't stay with each other, so the kids and I went to stay at my parents' house on September 12, 2016.

And that was the day that I decided to leave all drugs alone! The drugs were ruining my life—and not only mine. They were causing problems for anyone who cared about me! Mikey and I had not talked for two days, and on September 14, I got a call from a number I did not know. It was Mikey calling from jail! He was calling to tell me he was arrested for manufacturing and distributing meth!

That day, we picked up like nothing had ever happened between us, and I was there to support him through this time! As the days passed and my head cleared, I was able to see how much more to life there was than drugs! How good it felt to spend time with my kids and actually know what was going on! Mikey and I never really talked about God, but we'd both been raised in church-going families, as Mikey's dad was a pastor his whole life. So we both knew who God was! Well, the kids and I started going to church. Mikey and I started praying together on the phone, and I told Mikey we had to give it to God! What we were both going through was so much bigger than we were, and only God could and would get us through this dark place! I remember Mikey calling me from jail, telling me he was delivered. He'd just surrendered all in the shower! He said this was different than any other time before; this was it!

We were overwhelmed with excitement! Mikey had been locked up four months, and we both were four months clean and ready to start a new life together, allowing the Lord to work in us! He was getting released two days before my birthday on December 4, 2016, and we were just so happy to hug each other and be side by side that we stayed together the first two nights! The house we were living in was old and had black mold, and it was just not safe for us, so we knew we could not stay there. But we also had talked about how we wanted to live according to God's will and in that case living together just would not be right! So he stayed at his parents', and the kids and I stayed at my parents'. We were only five minutes from each other! When Sunday rolled around, we went to church and went up together and rededicated our lives to the lord! It was awesome! Since that day we are a year and half clean, still living separately and living our lives for the lord! My kids have seen the huge change that the lord has done in me and in us and how he has rebuilt our relationship! My boys often look at me and say, "Mom, I can't remember the last time you said a cuss word." I love hearing them tell me how proud they are of me! I can't express how grateful I am for everything the Lord has blessed me with in such a short time! He has blessed me with a job and given me a whole new attitude about life and who I am!

This past Christmas, I was able to get my kids everything they asked for on their Christmas list and not even have to stress about it! Because, when you're obedient in God's will, he does help provide! I have a good car that gets me back and forth, and I have money that I work for, so the kids and I are able to do things! I look back and can't thank the Lord enough for helping me get to where I am! I share my testimony because I thought I could never get out of my dark place. I thought there was no hope for me, but we serve an amazing God who still reveals things to me daily. When I find something bothering me or just feel like it's a bad day, I say a prayer and ask God to guide me in the right direction and just give me strength! We often think that, because we can't see God or see immediate answers to what we pray for, he is not there. But let me just tell you, as someone who was broken and lost, that he is a healer, a friend, a father, and so much more!

Lee Ann

Two years ago *today*, my baby girl stopped doing dope. Two years ago today, Ashley May was reborn. My daughter is a recovering addict. Her drug of choice was heroin. For ten years, heroin ruled her life. Heroin took her away from her family and her friends and led her straight to a personal *hell* that you cannot imagine. And it took us with her. I knew my baby girl would die. No question. And I was powerless to stop it. As parents, we are protectors of our babies. But I couldn't protect her from herself.

Every story of addiction is painful, scary, and seemingly hopeless. Ashley went all in with her addiction. She ran in Toledo with the gangs and did things she never thought she would do, all for the love of heroin. Her story is one of courage and strength. Her story is heartbreaking and inspiring all at the same time.

My daughter is strong. My daughter is courageous. My daughter is amazing. God is using her now to bring hope to others.

Ashley Raelynn, I love you. I am proud of you.

I am the mother of a two-year-clean recovering addict…and my child is a beast! A savage! A warrior! And she is kicking ass every day! You inspire me, Sis. You make me want to be a better person too. You have shown me what faith, courage, and strength are truly all about. You're my hero.

Love, Mom

> Recovery doesnt guarantee you anything other than a chance to build your life back better. It doesnt guarantee you health, wealth or happiness, however it does guarantee you the opportunity to achieve whatever area(s) you put the effort
>
> JR WEAVER

Timothy

My name is Timothy, I was born unto the flesh on December 11th, 1976, in a small east Kentucky town called Martin, approximately twenty miles from my hometown of Hindman. I take full responsibility for everything I'm about to tell you. It was no one's fault but my own. This was my path, my cross, and my journey. I had a pretty good childhood; I grew up in a family of six with one older brother and two older sisters. I am the baby boy of the family. My parents are both still living and married. I was a decent student, a decent looking kid, and I excelled at any sport I played and I was blessed to be coached by some very good men.

I had a heart of gold. I was very blessed right from the start, but Satan started plotting and deceiving me at a very young age. I did not see my blessings. I saw them as curses. I spent twenty-seven years of my life in active addiction, total chaos, and confusion. It started around the age of fourteen with a very bad social phobia that made it difficult for me to play sports and attend any large gatherings (sporting events). Around this time, I started experimenting with alcohol and pot. I "bought the lie" that alcohol soothed my social phobia, and I could still attend school functions and be relaxed. I thought it made me even more likable.

I was so confused about everything. I didn't understand or grasp the concept of life and all these crazy feelings and things going on around me, so I did what many kids do: I rebelled against almost everything that was right and of the light and welcomed sin into my life. I became an alcoholic (addict). I barely graduated high school and bounced around colleges until I met the mother of my two oldest children. I moved to Nicholasville, Kentucky and started working selling cars (the worst job in the world for someone with social phobia, go figure). I was twenty-three or twenty-four at this time. I was introduced to opiates and Xanax then, and this started another long and confusing season in my life.

As a child, all I could ever remember wanting was a happy family, to be a good daddy, and to make happy, healthy memories with them. That was not in God's plans for me at that time, and it almost destroyed me. I lost a piece of me around this time and am just now getting it back fifteen years later. After the divorce in 2005, I resigned from the postal service and moved back to eastern Kentucky to be closer to my children. I met the mother of my youngest daughter in 2006, and I prayed that this was my new chance at a happy family. Around this time, I was prescribed suboxone, clonazepam, and Neurontin by a doctor, and I started a ten-year addiction to these drugs. Yes, I am aware of the dangers of suboxone and the concept of trading one addiction for another (which is exactly what I did). But if used correctly (for a short period of time), I believe that it can help. I have no doubts that they saved my life and sustained me until I could find it within myself (God) to break free of that bondage. Had I not found suboxone and continued with the OxyContin/Xanax combination, I'm not sure if I would have made it to here, but I'm completely sure that God has the perfect plan.

    Without my addiction, I'd never been the man I was destined to be. I learned so much from that darkness. I learned not to judge, I learned just how important honesty is, I learned how important faithfulness is, and I learned about compassion and mercy and grace. On August 6, 2017, I was on day three of suboxone withdrawals, and I was in the middle of a methamphetamine addiction. I hadn't drunk alcohol in seven years or so because I was so unpredictable when I did. I would lose total control of myself; it has always been my kryptonite. That Saturday, Satan planted the seed of deception. He told me to go to the liquor store and buy a fifth of vodka "to ease the suboxone withdrawals." I had been entrusted to watch and protect my two darling daughters that weekend. I knew how important this job was, but I was struggling to care for myself. I was in a very dark place. I went downstairs and locked myself in the bathroom, like I always did, to hide and get high/drunk. My children were not aware of my addiction until toward the end. I drank the whole fifth. I was blacking in and out, and I can only remember bits and pieces. I texted my mom, brother, two sisters, and baby girl's momma, "I'm checking out, Love you."

    I proceeded to swallow over seventy muscle relaxers and lay down and waited to die. The only thing that had kept me alive for sixteen years was the thought of leaving my children with the burden of burying their daddy. I couldn't put that on them, and that night, I was not even aware of having children. It never crossed my mind to text or tell them bye. The first officer to arrive was a very brave and intelligent young man, with a heart of gold. I'd almost convinced him that everything was ok, and he was about to leave. I can remember my saving grace sobbing in the background, "Daddy, you're not ok! What did you do? Tell him the truth!" If she hadn't done what she'd done and the young cop had listened to me, I would have lain down that night, and those two babies would've woken to find their daddy cold.

    That wasn't God's plan, though. They called other officers in, and they placed me under arrest. I coded in the back of the cruiser on the way to the jail, which is a rock's throw from my old house. They dragged my lifeless body from the back of the car and started CPR in front of the jail. The paramedics arrived and took me to the ER, where they put me on life support. I was put in ICU. It was a joint effort, from my family making the correct phone calls to my daughter's intuition (my saving grace), to the police officers, to the EMTs, to the ER workers, to the ICU staff. Of course, the prayers and mercy and grace (God) helped. I could never repay any of you. All I can do is let all of you know that it was *not* in vain. By saving my physical body, you helped save a bunch of other people as well. If it saves just one, then it was all worth it. I'll dedicate the rest of my life to helping others by showing them the way out of that darkness.

I didn't get straight by going to church. I didn't get straight by going to rehab. I didn't get straight by going to NA meetings. I got straight by earnest and sincere prayer and by throwing myself into the Word. If God can restore a completely broken and "hopeless addict" and bring him back from the brink of insanity and chaos into complete sobriety in 365 days, what can he do for you?

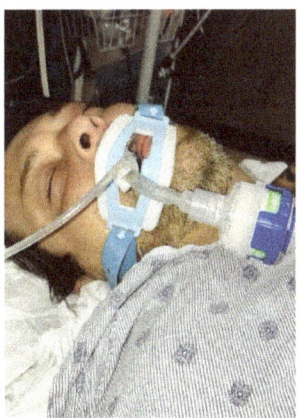 

Maura

Hi. I've never been a fan of tough love when it comes to addiction. Even detaching with love—I understand it but don't like the term. We all have our own way. I'm not capable of "detaching." I don't want to detach. I'm at a place where I want to enjoy each and every minute I have with my son. He is currently in recovery, but when and if he relapses, I still need him in my life. Boundaries, yes—but I will always be here for him on some level. I don't think that is enabling either. I think it's necessary for me. Yep, for *me*. This is about me too. In the past, I worried about doing the "right" thing. It took me a long time to be true to myself and do what felt right to me, even if it went against professional advice. If there was a solid one-size-fits-all answer, the choice would be simple. None of this is simple, but my love for him is and that's all I have to give. It's something he never need doubt.

Emily

This has been my hardest year so far, I believe, but I have learned the most valuable life lessons. When I went to treatment in February 2016, I was so broken down and battered that I completely and utterly had just given up. I did not have one single ounce of will left in me. The more people tried to make me see all these things to live for, the more it just made me want them and myself to die. I had already tried to get clean dozens of times over the years. I had gone cold turkey plenty of times in my own home, sweating toxins through a new set of sheets each day, I had been to detox facilities, inpatient treatment programs, sober-living houses, IOP, twelve-step meetings, the whole works, but nothing ever stuck. I had kind of made peace with the notion that nothing was going to work and that was ok. Getting and staying clean and sober was the hardest thing in the world for me to do, and I was so sick of trying and failing that my philosophy had simply become this: I wasn't going to try anymore. I had absolutely no expectations for myself and could not give two shits about anyone's pompous-ass expectations for me.

Over the years, during my periods of brief clean times, it would be like a fog lifting, and there were these small little windows of clarity, where I would emerge and finally decide to get cleaned up, shower, brush my teeth, etc. You see, when you're strung out, personal hygiene is the first to go. Sometimes it would be weeks since I had last looked at myself in a mirror, and when I finally would, I would hardly recognize the person staring back at me. My face looked foreign, my complexion had a yucky yellowish tint to it, and my body was thin and gaunt. I would peer into eyes so lost, searching for the slightest glint of familiarity. You can only imagine all the lives I had lived and the sights I had seen. I would reflect and process my situation, and it was clear that drugs were doing horrible things to my life.

As each year progressed, I could see a little bit more of every aspect of my life getting stripped away, but I would never gain a single thing. I was taking one step forward and two steps backward. Never moving forward or progressing toward anything of significance or means. By 2016, I had ruined my health, my wealth, my well-being, and my prosperity. I'd lost two cars, a $28 per hour job at my dad's business, a boyfriend of five years, two dogs, multiple friendships, and even the trust of most of my family. I had been in three treatment facilities and jail. I'd had multiple run-ins with the law and had been in and out of the hospital for months. My phone would hardly ring, and I only used it to contact my dealer.

The support system I once had slowly drifted away. At first, my family was a *huge* support system and stuck by my side when I first tried to get help. But the longer they remained on my deranged roller coaster ride of addiction that flipped and turned and somersaulted, the faster they wanted to get off and never get on again. I thought it was ride or die until the end. More like they just left me to crash and burn. What had happened to my support system? Well, some I think I threw off. Others got tired of my same never-ending shit. Some just grew bored of it, and some got physically ill, literally. My addiction had highs that were always too short lived, and then the lows dipped into the deepest pits of Hades. Drugs and alcohol stole my soul, turned tricks in my mind, painted my heart as black as coal, and left only a shell of a person that I almost lost permanently.

The past couple Christmases have been difficult for me, as well as for my family. First, let me say this: my family is a pretty chaotic bunch, and we will end up doing something drastic and epic that it is one for the history books. So, I guess I would've been shocked if the holiday season went off without a hitch. Whether it be jail, rehab, cops, guns, fist fights, a pregnancy, stolen property, drinking, drug dealing, death, fires, riots—you name it, and it's probably not too far-fetched for our family.

On Christmas Eve 2014, I was arrested and spent the night in jail. I was bailed out on Christmas day and came straight home and stayed strung out while gripping a shotgun under the Christmas tree. Then Christmas Eve 2015,

I got completely trashed; had a huge knockdown, drag-out fight with my brother; then got dropped off on the front doorsteps of a treatment facility, holding a small plastic bag full of belongings. I woke up in their parking lot later in the night and somehow ending up back in the hospital for the fourth time that year. My pancreas, liver, and kidneys were shutting down, and my body was literally giving up on me. The doctors told me that my organs would continue to shut down and I may not live to see Christmas 2016, if I did not stop all the drugs I was shooting, snorting, popping, smoking, along with all the alcohol I would drown myself in from sunup until sundown. My continued lifestyle of debauchery had been killing and robbing me of any and all signs of health, prosperity, and happiness for so many years, and it had finally caught up to me and was quite literally going to kill me. I would spend weeks in a hospital bed connected to IVs and pumps, just waiting to die. I hated leaving the hospital to come back home because that I meant I would have to leave my pain pump, which always kept enough medicine coursing through my body to keep me in a comatose state.

Instead of lessening the pain to any degree, I was only causing more within and around myself. I was trying too hard to conceal, kill, hide from, or wallow in all that hurt me and touched my soft spots deep inside. I was told I would die if I couldn't find it in me to *want* to live. The deeper you dig a hole, the harder it is to climb out. Well, I had gotten so comfortable down in the hole I'd dug that I simply crouched down and called it home. Frankly, I didn't even want to try to come out because I knew it would be too much work. It was so much easier for me to admit defeat and just keep killing myself than it was to try and fight to save myself. Dying was easy. I knew I could do it. Hell, I had been doing it for years. It was the living I didn't know if I could handle. I believe now, though; I can feel the biggest highs without even having to get high from drugs because I have felt the lowest of lows. I know the difference between being alive and *feeling* truly alive. I have no idea what I was so scared of for so many years, but it's not only easy; it's a lot of fun.

I am proud to announce it wasn't me that ruined this last Christmas, but I found out that my ex-fiancé had died of an overdose a week before, and then my brother did not spend Christmas with us once again due to his own addiction, which he's been battling for the past ten years. Since then, he has been arrested three times, spent multiple months in jail, and detoxed on his cell floor, with not one friend or relative posting a bond. But he has continually been released on charges and court orders to stay at state-funded rehabs. Then my mom gave him yet another chance to live at home, and he relapsed within two weeks and got kicked out on Christmas Eve after I found a syringe on the bathroom floor.

Five years ago, my brother was in college. He had his own condo, a job working for the family business, a company truck, friends and family that he could rely on. Now everything he owns is able to fit in a backpack. He has sold, pawned, and traded everything of value, including everything my dad left him when he died. He has even traded everything down to his shoes. He only owns one pair of cheap sneakers, once a drug dealer's, that he got after trading every pair of Nikes he had for a small amount of heroin. This is proof that addiction can steal everything from someone, leaving them bare, stripped down to the bone.

My brother is the one who introduced me to heroin, as well crack, dealers, and the worst streets in Memphis, streets that someone like me should never be caught dead on. He also taught me the real ins and outs of how to shoot up. I hadn't used in almost two years, so my mind started racing a million miles an hour when I found that needle on the bathroom floor. My hands got clammy, I started sweating, and my body started shaking. I felt overwhelming emotions inside of me, but I felt mostly anger and rage because I felt he did this on purpose just to try to fuck with me and my sobriety. Misery does love company, but in my brother's case, he takes as many innocent victims as possible and holds them prisoner, inflicting pain and spreading hatred around like a contagious disease that breeds such ugliness. The truth: hurt people hurt people.

I remembered everything I loved about the drug, but then I remembered everything I despised about it. I thought of everything I'd let drugs take away from me. Everything I had given away and the power it had over me and could easily have again. And then I thought of all the strength I had now and how powerful *that* was, and I focused on that feeling only. He eventually told my mom that he had, in fact, relapsed and had been trying to overdose and kill himself. Later that night, she asked me when I thought we would get a call or a knock on the door to let us know he was dead. She said she feared it every day. She does not deserve this.

I have learned this much: just because we feel pain doesn't mean we have to be pain. I also realize now that much of what used to hurt me had to do with the years I'd spent hating myself, instead of loving the person I was. I put my soul through hell and then hated how pathetic my life had become. The strength I have gained through sobriety reminds me how much wickedness my addiction caused.

I have been beaten down, bruised, and cried more this year than any other year, including the year my dad died of cancer, but I have also stood proud, smiled, and laughed uncontrollably and senselessly until my abs hurt. I have met the most wonderful and supportive groups of people and friends, rather than making enemies or using others only as a means to an end for my own selfish gain. I have hugged the most beautiful souls and offered a helping hand to those in need instead of sticking knives in others' backs or resolving spats with fists pounding flesh. I have had deep and moving conversations with caring, like-minded individuals, and when I said, "I love you," I really did mean it, instead of spitting language venom, cutting someone down in size, and screaming, "Fuck you!"

I prayed harder than I ever have, begging him for help, strength, and courage, asking for healing hands over all those sick and suffering, praising him for every single blessing he has granted in my life. I started reminding myself that it's ok to make mistakes. I still continue to make mistakes, a lot of them, and I am indeed ok with it. Practicing patience. Expressing feelings is still difficult. Cherish the little things. Slowing down. Life is so fleeting.

Spread smiles, compliment others, share big warm hugs, and value them when they're given in return, knowing the smallest gestures can make someone's day. Recognize how special family is during the good times, as well as the bad. Give more power to love over hate. I'm improving on my listening—listening more to others, to God, and to myself. Positive vibes can send the most vital signs. I remind myself time and time again of my sense of self-worth, but I also remember others. I'm not too hard on myself, but I also recognize when improvements are needed. I've rediscovered a whole new me and all the strong qualities I hold.

I vow to love life and try to be the best possible human I can be for the good of mankind. I've made peace with the mistakes of my past. I realize the magnitude of forgiveness. I've practiced forgiveness and am still practicing forgiveness. I've learned that honesty is the best policy. So I got honest with myself, like real honest, and then I irrevocably devoted myself to loving every single morsel, drop, and square inch of my beautifully fucked up story, and in doing so, I found my best version of myself. Then I vowed to value myself that I am worthy of saving. I am worthy of love. I am worthy of forgiveness. I am worthy of second chances, third chances, or however many chances I damn well want. I am worthy of kindness. I am worthy of all the goodness in the world. And most importantly, I am worthy of not settling for what I don't want out of life or in my life. I am finding there is beauty in flaws. I keep no reservations. I hold no judgments. I take pride in each battle wound, bruise, and scar. I humble myself by being my number-one biggest fan, embracing my faults and all. I am so blessed to be alive and breathing today, and I continue to look forward to everything this life has in store for me.

Prince

I stopped by to drop some hope for all those battling with this disease of addiction and testify that we do recover. This is the first time in recovery that I have finally chosen to surrender my broken, addicted life into the hands of God. I've come to the conclusion that I can't do this on my own or by using God to help me accomplish my own purposes and ambitions in recovery. I have to live a life completely surrendered to God and allow God to use me as a vessel, as an instrument of his light and love to accomplish the purposes of my creation. On November 25, 2017, I died from an overdose after two years clean and four months as an active user. God gave me a second opportunity at life to live for him and share my message of hope with everyone I encounter. Since then, he has been reshaping my existence here on earth and using me in ways that I only used to dream of. He has restored every relationship with family and friends and healed my broken heart. Today, I am four months clean, serving God with my life and preparing a speech for a toast at my brother's wedding. Life is greater than anything I ever could imagine or create in my own power. Surrender your life and this disease to God one day at a time and allow him to transform your existence!

Debra

Six years ago today, on April 10, 2012, homeless, hopeless and broken, I came to, alone in a motel. I didn't know where I was or what had happened. Drugged and robbed but alive. I heard a voice clearly saying, "Go. It's done; we can do it; you're not alone."

It was at that moment that I made a decision to choose *life*. The next day, I said goodbye to only one person. I said I was going away to change my life. I would not be back. I made my way to a detox on Easter Eve. They had no beds and told me to come back tomorrow. I told them, "No, I can't leave because I won't make it back."

They put me in a room with a love seat. They said to take a nap and that they would be back. They forgot about me until the next day. On Easter, I awoke and went to find a bathroom. The lady at the desk was amazed to see me. A bed had just come open. I have never looked back. Only when I will use my experiences to inspire hope to another hopeless, broken individual like me. Today, I follow the voice of God that led me safely out of there. I trust, believe, and have experienced one miracle after the other. I am so humbled and grateful today for my recovery and all the amazing people in my life that love me unconditionally. I'm extremely blessed for a life so abundant. *His* promises are true to life, so I will continue to listen for God's voice. In the name of Yeshiva, amen.

A Letter from a Mom

Where do I start? I am a mom of four. Also, we have four grandchildren. My eldest daughter began her battle with opioid addiction after she left home, leaving her son behind at the age of two. We still have him. We knew she was partying. We had no clue what the drug was and didn't find out until two years later that it was heroin.. I am guilty of my own addictions, nicotine and caffeine. But otherwise, we taught our kids about properly prescribed medications and doing your own research when any doctor suggested any medicines. For the most part, our household only uses antibiotic meds when absolutely necessary. We can't blame the medical community for our daughter's addiction. She chose using. We can never understand why. We loved her through it all, and she set herself onto the recovery journey twice. The second time, she remained clean—straight edge—for almost a year. She was in meetings a minimum of nine sessions a week. She was treasure chair in one group. In July last year, she was elected to open a new recovery home for women in that area. We had sent her to another state to get clean, and there were too many people at home she was determined to cut ties from.

Three months later, she slipped and used once. The coroner said it was evident it was an isolated use. Not enough heroin in her body to have hurt a fly. The Fentanyl it was cut with ended her life. I've been trying to do what I can to help other parents. Other addicts. Others trying to recover. I've met so many who have burned bridges, and I have some difficulty relating to family members who write off their loved ones over addictions. I love people where they are. I don't have any regrets. No guilt over the relationship I had with my girl. I know ours was repaired, and we were in a good place up until she was gone. I'm looking forward to doing something in my community to help make a difference. I talk every single day to "kids" that struggle, and I just try to listen and encourage them. They do reach out sometimes, and I just try to be a source of love.

I DIDN'T COME THIS FAR TO ONLY COME THIS FAR.

> Recovery doesnt guarantee you anything other than a chance to build your life back better. It doesnt guarantee you health, wealth or happiness, however it does guarantee you the opportunity to achieve whatever area(s) you put the effort
>
> JR WEAVER

Jasmine

My name is Jasmine, and I am a drug addict. Sure, what meets the eye does not look like a "drug addict," but trust me; two years ago, I fit the physical description of what a "drug addict" would look like. Two years ago, I was homeless, I didn't eat, and I was covered in filth. When I took my sandals off, you could see the dirt caked between my toes. My appearance was dirty and dingy; my hair and body were contaminated with a mixture of grease and dirt. I stayed in a broken-down home filled with mold. If you don't have experience with living in an environment that is covered in mold, let me explain. The home I was in had a constant horrible stench, and I was always unable to breath while I was inside it. There was never a source of fresh water or any of the common extremities that we take for granted on a daily basis. Outside, we had a children's swimming pool that only was filled with water from the rain. That is where I would occasionally bathe. To say that I felt and believed that I was less than a human being is an understatement. I hated life, and I hated myself.

I did not end up in recovery because I wanted to, and I certainly did not believe that I was deserving of a happy and purposeful life. I came to recovery because people loved me and believed in me. No matter how far down the scale I had gone (and trust me I had gone pretty low), for some reason, people gave me the love that I was incapable of giving myself.

I came in weak and broken. I could not make eye contact with other humans. I was so consumed by the shame I felt. I quickly learned what addiction really is. I learned why people loved me no matter what I did and why people continued to show up in my life and show compassion. I learned that, for most people, addiction really has nothing to do with the physical dependency, like we were all taught to think. I was taught that drugs are bad and the people that do them were bad too. Turns out this is not true. Not everyone who does drugs becomes a drug addict. Actually, very few people become physically addicted, and furthermore, some of those people that become physically addicted, once separated from the drug, are able to put it down and not destroy their life. Why not me? Why was I so different than most of the world's population?

From my earliest memories, I felt alone. I don't have happy childhood memories. I'm sure that there are some, but that is not how I remember my childhood. I remember having a nervous disposition, always being afraid, not having friends, and generally being completely miserable in my own skin as child. This carried over into my teenage years and into my adulthood. I am a trauma survivor and experienced lots of heartbreaking and soul-draining abuse during my early childhood. I experienced things that would strip any child of their innocence. Is this why I became a drug addict? Some people would say yes. I would say that this plays a part in why I became a drug addict but is not the sole reason for my addiction.

Drugs and alcohol took all of this away. It took away all the pain, self-hatred, insecurity, loneliness. Drugs were my solution. They made everything better. Of course, I very quickly became physically addicted. Every time I was able to free myself of the physical component, I somehow would end up picking drugs back up, despite knowing the consequences of my addiction. The truth that I learned about addiction was that drugs were not my problem. How I felt, who I was internally, was my problem!

I am highly favored by the Universe (in my opinion). God put the most beautiful, nonjudgmental, and loving people in my life. Those people carried me for the first couple months of my sobriety. I quickly found my place in a twelve-step recovery program and found what I would call "a relationship with a higher power." I had and still have the most amazing leaders, who share their wisdom and guidance with me. I remain humble and teachable. I have set right many wrongs, and I am still working toward complete salvation. I know that, no matter what the trouble or situation that arises in my life may be, there is a solution for it. I am no longer plagued with impending doom. As I write this, I have the biggest smile and tears flowing down my checks. I am honestly and truly happy today! I can allow myself to be happy, and it is beautiful. I have goals and dreams. I have friends. For the first time in my life, I actually have healthy relationships with others. I am still working on repairing relationships with my family, but most importantly, I have a relationship with myself, and I am no longer a stranger in my own body.

Today, I celebrate two years clean and sober. This would not be possible without God and the endless amount of love from others.

> Changing from a 'victim mentality' to a 'winning mentality' is the game changer.
>
> JR WEAVER

> THE BRAVEST THING I
> HAVE EVER DONE WAS
> ASKING FOR HELP
> AGAINST A ENEMY
> THAT KNEW ME BETTER
> THAN I KNEW MYSELF.
>
> JR WEAVER

> Easier to stay addicted off the past than it is to stay sober off what you did yesterday. Irony.
>
> JR WEAVER

Cheryle

As June 28 approaches every year, I always think back to what it was like on June 27, 1989, the day before I got into recovery.

I was twenty-nine years old. I now have twenty-nine years in recovery, and it's amazing. Back then, I had no idea how to handle the ups and downs that life throws at you. I didn't even have the words to communicate that I didn't believe in myself.

What I did have was a two-and-a-half-year-old precious baby boy, and I didn't want him to grow up seeing his mother struggling the way that I was.

When I finally had the courage to ask for help, help was available immediately. I'm not sure that, if they had said, "Come tomorrow" or "Make an appointment," I would be where I am today. I'm pretty confident I would've changed my mind. And what a different, shorter life I may have had.

I got seven days of detox, twenty-eight days of inpatient treatment, and then a year of outpatient treatment in the evenings so I could continue to work. The last twenty-nine years have gone by like a flash. I attended twelve-step meetings regularly. They taught me to keep coming, to be on time, to show up and do for others, and many, many other skills that I would need to be successful in my life.

I raised my child in recovery. I made some mistakes for sure, but I was always doing my best, which got better with time. Today I am so absolutely proud of the man that my son has become. For a long time, early in my recovery, he was the reason I stayed. Eventually, I stayed in recovery because it was good for me.

Recovery has taught me so many things. Most importantly, it has shown me how to be the best me I can be every day. I live every day being honest, treating people with respect, and above all, living with gratitude.

A Mother

I was sitting alone—and obviously stricken—in a crowded courtroom five years ago while my beloved daughter was being handcuffed and remanded to jail after sentencing to await a bed for treatment. She turned my way as she was led out of the room and screamed—expletive deleted—at me. It was horrible, and I just sat there, unable to move. An elderly man, a complete stranger, took my hand and pressed a folded piece of paper into it. I didn't read it until I had somehow made it to my car. In it was her purse, and in the purse was her rig with a full syringe. Maybe if she'd not been sent to jail, that would have been her last day on earth. I read the note he gave me every day. She is still with us. Struggling but here. Where there is life, there is hope.

The Addiction Manifesto

Kay
A message of hope. My boy is now twenty years old. His journey into substance abuse started when he was thirteen. Weed, pills, and finally heroin. Multiple treatment centers (eight to nine). Our life turned into chaos, confusion, and disorder. I can remember the fear every morning as I went to knock on his door to wake him up for school. Would he be alive or dead? It was a total feeling of helplessness. He had been to the best treatment centers and had a family that loved and supported him, but it was never enough. Search warrants at my house were not foreign. We finally sent him out of state to Wilderness Treatment Center in Montana. After two months, he left on a direct flight to Los Angeles to sober living at New Life House. After sixteen months at NLH, he graduated!

While there, he graduated from high school, got his first driver's license (he was a proficient driver because he'd taken my car out many times when I was asleep!), bought his first car, and got his first apartment with two other NLH graduates. He is preparing to take his test to get his real-estate license. So don't lose hope. He is out there in the big, bad world now, and I pray every day that he stays the course. This is the next chapter in his journey. Please keep him in your thoughts and prayers. I miss him every day, but I know that he is with an amazing brotherhood in recovery. He is giving back to the house, mentoring the new members. I'm a very proud and grateful mama! God is good!

Bobbie
If a mother's prayers get answered, this kid (who is now a twenty-eight-year-old man) is going to come out of this bigger and better and stronger than ever. If a mother's prayers get answered, his struggles with addiction will help him carry an important message to other addicts. If a mother's prayers get answered, he will find a path he can stay on. If a mother's prayers get answered, he will get to enjoy his daughter growing up the way we enjoyed him. If a mother's prayers get answered, I won't be burying my son.

Taylor

Two years, twenty-four months, 730 days, 1,051,200 minutes, 63,072,000 seconds. That's how long it's been since I have picked up a drink or a drug! Does that sound crazy to you? Because it sounds crazy to me! If you had told me two years ago that my life would be what it is today, I wouldn't have believed you. I would have sold myself so short.

I have grown tremendously within the past two years. I have endured loss, pain, and heartache and stayed sober through it. That in itself is *huge*; I used to use those as excuses to get high. I would feel justified doing the things I was doing because I had a "poor me" mentality. Selfishness and self-centeredness were the root of all my problems. I was always thinking about myself in every single situation, never able to see or hear the people around me or care. I was unable to maintain a job because, at the first sign of withdrawals, I would call in sick and not care about the consequences. Jumping from one restaurant job to another, only to last a couple of months—sometimes not even months but only weeks.

I was constantly putting myself *and* others in questionable and dangerous situations, not giving a shit about the outcome. All I gave a shit about was that next high, that next ten-second rush, when really, nine times out of ten, I wouldn't even get it. That's the insanity of this disease, though; I was chasing a feeling that was going to kill me. It was just a matter of when. I was in and out of abusive relationships with drug dealers because it was what was convenient. I had no self-worth or any type of standards. If you sold drugs or had what I wanted/needed, I clung to you like a parasite.

That's exactly what I was: a parasite. Sucking the life out of everyone around me with my misery and sickness. The mental and emotional torment I put myself through for years is the definition of insanity. I was doing the same thing over and over, expecting different results, and never once did I get them. It just continued to get progressively worse over the years. It was so dark and lonely, and the deeper into it I got, the dimmer the light at the end of the tunnel got. By the end, I was to a point where I accepted being a junkie and was okay with dying. As a matter of fact, I welcomed it. Dying seemed better than feeling what I was feeling and doing what I was doing. That is no way for anyone to live. It breaks my heart watching the people I love struggle and knowing that they have the option to surrender; all they need to do is reach out and ask for help. Getting clean is definitely not easy and probably one of the hardest and most emotionally draining things I have ever done, but it was *so worth it*. You are so worth it. Life is so worth it. After a series of overdoses, I am still here and breathing. God gave me another chance; he knew I had a purpose in this lifetime. I'll never understand why I got so many chances and my best friends didn't. Why God chose to take them and not me. And the truth is, it's not my job to understand. My job is to fulfill God's purpose and keep spreading love, light, and hope to those around me.

Over the past two years, I have gained so much. I am beyond blessed for the path I was put on. Today I am employable and work with an amazing group of women who encourage me and inspire me daily, doing what I love. Today I am a loving and reliable daughter, sister, and friend. Today I am a loving and faithful girlfriend in a beautiful relationship with a man who has shown me what true unconditional love is. Today, not only am I a dog mom, but I will officially be a mother to a beautiful baby boy, come January. Today I have learned to love myself for exactly who I am today, I have learned to be honest no matter what, I have learned that I have to get uncomfortable to be comfortable, and I have gained a sense of peace and quiet in my own mind.

I am able to show up for others today and be of service. I am surrounded with love and inspiration today. I have found a spiritual program of action and have gone through the steps necessary to achieve and maintain my sobriety. I feel like I am making a difference today. And for that, I will be forever grateful. Here's to many more years of living this beautiful life, God willing.

It begins with you believing that you deserve better, whether its a better life, better relationship or just a better you. You are the only person that has the power to change you, or break you.

JR WEAVER

Nika

My name is Nika, and I am an alcoholic and drug addict. I have been clean and sober since February 28, 2017.

Recovery has been, undoubtedly, the hardest thing I have ever had to do. I thought that, once I had gotten rid of the drugs and alcohol, that I would be ok. That has been so far from the truth. I have kicked and screamed my way through this past year. I have thought about killing myself, blade in hand. I have almost thrown in the towel more than once—and in more ways than one. I have stopped seeking God. I have cried to the point of shaking and sweating with fear of how I'm going to get through this. I have questioned my sanity—and if I even have any. I have questioned my life and my worth more times than I can count. I have wanted to quit, and I have wanted to die. But every time, my God's grace has been upon me and pushed me through, to this day. I am a year sober, and I have hit enough pain to start looking internally and discover who I truly am. I keep pushing. I know there is a way out, and I remain faithful. In my heart, I know that I am truly blessed, and for that, I am grateful.

When you stop to write down your recovery story about where you've been, where your currently at, and where your planning to go, you realize the power of recovery. Your eyes are open to the blessings that sobriety brings to you. Bouncing back from the hell that we once accepted as normal during our addiction and living a life worth living—that is incredible! We can take pride in what we're doing, and other people will notice too. Stop and take a minute to appreciate that it is not easy to admit defeat to addiction and then walk away a winner. We admitted defeat, and we won back our life. Make sense? It takes a tremendous amount of courage, strength, and guts to reach out for help. That was the hardest step for someone like me, but the gratitude I now feel toward those who helped me find the way back is something that I will always cherish. If you have learned something or enjoyed this book, please be sure to leave a review where you picked it up. Thank you for reading this, and I really hope this has opened your mind to make some changes.

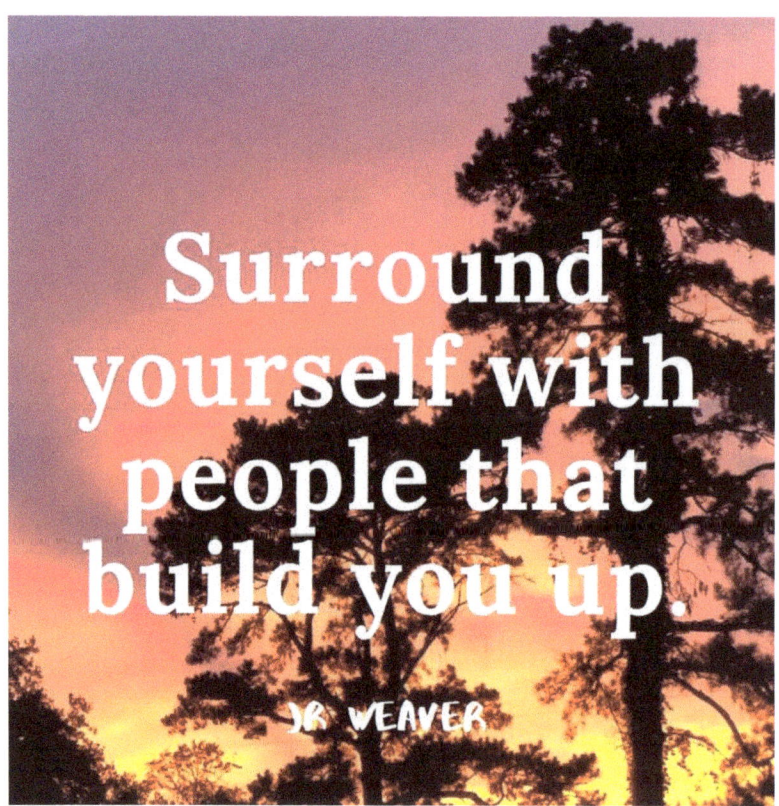

The power of words. Way back when I started writing this book, I had one goal, and that goal was to write about anything and everything that would help keep me sober. The more I've written, the more my goals have expanded. My new goal is to help keep others sober or help bring them closer to choosing sobriety. The current system (rehabs, detoxes, AA/NA, and SMART Recovery meetings) is a great place to start your journey to recovery. It gives each of us the tools and knowledge to build on. A foundation for our recovery to grow. I know that AA/NA meetings were a great place for me to hear things that I personally needed to hear, but it might not be the thing that does it for you. Maybe it's the people there, or maybe it's the whole spiritual higher power thing that turns you off from their program. If that's the case, then you should at least try out the SMART Recovery Program. It stands for Self-Management and Recovery Training, and it's another option that offers free, self-empowering, mutual-help groups for learning how to beat your addictions. Celebrate Recovery is another program offered by local churches that will help us learn to live sober; it's a more religious-based group.

Boom! And just like that, life has purpose. Let go of the negative habits that "take" from you every day. Do things that feed your soul and learning to accept your new life isn't going to be all tacos and sun-shiny days. Life isn't always fair; we all must deal with it the best we can. Unless your last name is Kardashian, you will face adversity. We will face challenges, but we learn from them, and we will grow. We don't run on self-will; when we do, we lose sight of what we've learned in recovery. We are now faced with redefining ourselves, our goals. Take that hill and take that mountain; first figure out what that hill or mountain is. Family? Health? Personal success? Our goals may change over time, but that's ok. As long as we continue on this golden path, we'll be just fine.

Life isn't going to cater to us. We have to want it. We must put forth the effort, and we must not be afraid to ask for help. Remember that Rome wasn't built in a day, so be ready to roll up those sleeves and put in some work. Rebuilding ourselves isn't a quick fix, but each day going forward, we will be happier. How do I know this? Because I'm living proof.

> Cause at the end of the day,
> You gotta love you some you.
>
> JR WEAVER

The struggle is real. We're taking back our lives one day at a time! Our enemy wants to enslave us until it destroys us! Addiction doesn't give a damn about what side of the tracks you live on, the color of your skin, or what religion you belong to. Its mission is to use us until we die a lonely, miserable, isolated death. It can blind us to the destruction and utter chaos it's creating in our life, tearing us away from our true friends and families too. We face the hard truth somewhere during this time. Unfortunately, some of us have to hit our rock bottom, and even sadder, some of us won't ever have another day.

We must learn to *fight back*! We must learn to *take back our lives*! We have to believe that we can win this fight, right now, each day, or even each hour. We must channel the same energy we used to feed our addictions into feeding our recoveries! Rain or snow never stopped us during our addiction, so why should it stop us in our recovery? We must dedicate our days to getting better, to going the extra mile to help others; that will also help us. This is a life-or-death battle. If we fail, we may not get another chance. That's real. You have to embrace your recovery and keep it the front of your priorities. Recovery saves us from going back out there, and I know I am finally happy today because I value my sobriety. One day at a time. It takes one small spark to start this recovery revolution. Let's get our lives back and help others get theirs back too! Want it and go make it happen.

There is no one program that fits all in recovery. Try to find out what works best for you and do more of that. Recovery isn't a race; it's more of a marathon, one day at a time. Focus on that, and your life will blossom.

Warning: Speed Bumps

If only real life came with warning signs, eh? Recovery from addiction is a road filled with potholes. We get so focused on staying clean that we have a tendency to miss the obstacles and detours that life throws in our path; we get blindsided. Life isn't going to be easy for us. We're basically starting over, and some of us may have lost everything too. Starting over at forty-seven and rebuilding my life was a tough choice to make, but destroying myself with drugs or alcohol was no longer a viable option. I could continue to self-medicate until I burned everything I valued to the ground, or I could own my mistakes and get help. I chose the hard road: recovery. Recovery to regain control of my life. The early days had me questioning everything. I didn't know if I was going to make it. A few times, I almost did tap out, but I stayed focused and trusted the process. I walked miles, I rode buses, and I never gave up hope that I could turn my life around. Slowly, things got better. I got a car, I got accepted into a great hospital-training program at the VA, and I got my family back. Each step forward was a blessing, and it got easier after all the hardships and challenges that couldn't break me. I wanted my life back. One of my earliest goals was hitting that first year of sobriety. I'm about nine days away, and I'm like, "Wow, what an incredible year for this guy—the guy who, one time, believed he couldn't sober up, who believed he was 'done' and destined for prison or being found dead in a ditch."

That's the miracle of recovery—seeing the blessings of things happening that you didn't believe could happen. I'm proud of where I stand today, and if this guy (me) can turn his life around, then anybody can. Trust the process, put forth the effort, and get your life back! Addiction doesn't care about you; it only cares about what you can do for it. Your family and true friends want you back.

> The biggest challenge ahead is between the 'old' you and the 'new' you, be very careful which side you give the bullets.
>
> JR WEAVER

> BECAUSE AT THE END OF THE DAY ALL THE SUPPORT IN THE WORLD DOESN'T MATTER IF YOU DON'T WANT TO CHANGE.
>
> *JR Weaver*

> Relapse isn't a option for me, it wouldn't be just for a nite or a weekend binge, it'd be 6 months long and i'd lose everything in the process, and lets not forget the felonies.
>
> JR WEAVER

> I had to survive my worst to find my best.
>
> JR WEAVER

> The day you accept the truth about addiction and the role it's played in destroying your life is the day you finally realize it never loved you. Want to know who does? Your friends and family, your children, your dog or cat, they never gave up on you.
>
> JR WEAVER

> GETTING SOBER CHANGED MY LIFE, FINDING RECOVERY SAVED MY LIFE.
>
> JR WEAVER

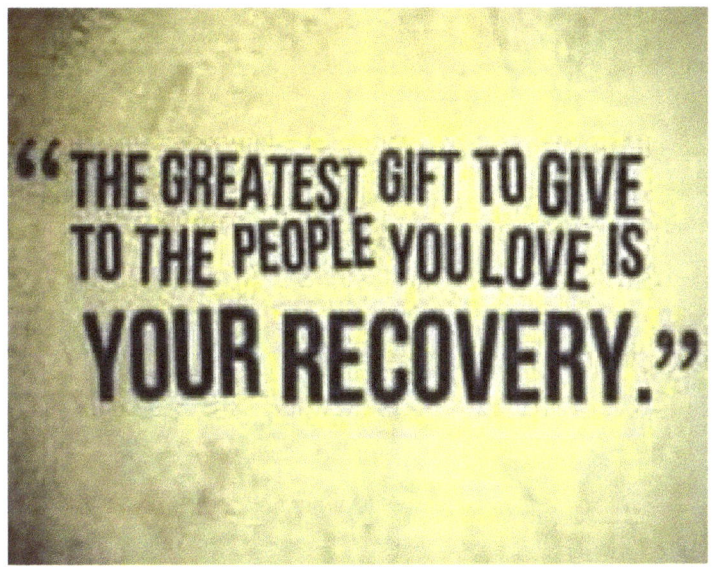

"THE GREATEST GIFT TO GIVE TO THE PEOPLE YOU LOVE IS YOUR RECOVERY."

PERSONAL THANKS

Thanks to the awesome team at Charleston County Drug Court for giving me a chance to have a life. Special thanks to John Palmer, Ms. Jackie for enlightening my mind, Karen Barker for the superstar legal support, and Debbie Walker and Judges Condin, Currie and Kouten for being patient with me and allowing me this opportunity to get better.

I know I have been blessed with a second chance at life through drug court, and what you have done to help me will never be forgotten.

Thanks to the team at the Ralph H. Johnson VAMC for building the foundation that my recovery is built on. Special thanks to Lauren Nelson, Tyrone, Mike, Meredith Miller, Stacey Patterson, Dr. Braxton, Dr. Lazano, and the rest of the great staff. You deserve much more credit for all the work you do with veterans. You are appreciated! We may not always "get the message" right away, but thanks to you, we have the tools to deal with life on life's terms! Thanks!

Thanks to everyone who helped donate their own personal stories of recovery. Your stories of inspiration are testimony that recovery works and that we all can have that life that we want, free from addiction! Keep coming back!

Thanks to my second family, my cyber family, my incredible Facebook family! My cyber family is credited with restoring my sanity back when my mind was weak and addiction was taking control. I probably wouldn't be writing this story without my Facebook family's unwavering support; they were truly a source of strength for me. They had my back when the real world was ready to give up on me. I love my cyber family, and I am grateful to have met such awesome friends online.

Thank you, Carrie Smith, for inspiring me to dig deeper and keeping me focused on my recovery. I don't know if I would have been able to finish this book without you.

Thank you for reading this! Hopefully, this book will help inspire and motivate you to find what works for you in your own recovery. Feel free to pass this book along to somebody who might need it. Good luck on your own journey to recovery. Please leave a review and spread the word!

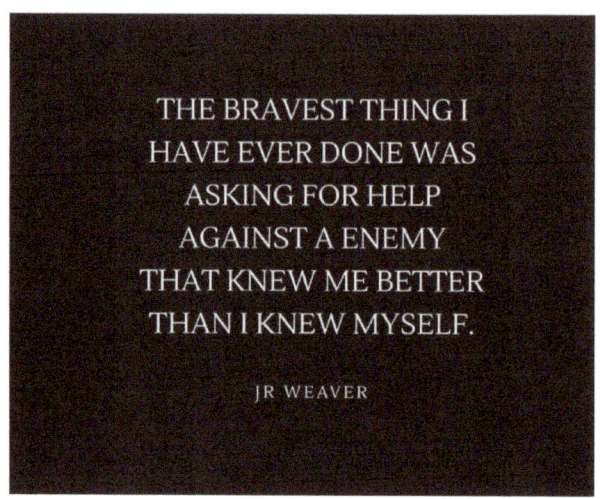

9-12-20: Our first ever Recovery Revolution "Walk and Talk"

> **WANT TO ELEVATE YOUR RECOVERY? ADD GOD TO YOUR SQUAD.**
>
> JR Weaver

The Addiction Manifesto

www.wakeupcarolina.org

www.thehopeproject.cc

> The power of your story has the juice to change lives. A person gets their life back, a mom gets her son or daughter back, a child gets their mommy or daddy back.
>
> JR WEAVER

Lightning Source UK Ltd.
Milton Keynes UK
UKHW022147210322
400390UK00006B/396